THE CARAVAN PILGRIM

The Caravan on the Road.

THE
CARAVAN PILGRIM

BY

PETER F. ANSON

With a Foreword
By
COMPTON MACKENZIE
and 56 full page illustrations by the Author.

HEATH CRANTON Limited,
6 Fleet Lane, London, E.C.4.

First published in 1938.

Made and printed in Great Britain for Heath Cranton Limited by
A. Dyer, Eaton Bray and London.

To
ANTHONY ROWE

Dear Tony,

I could not very well dedicate this book to anyone but yourself, for without your practical help and co-operation it could never have been written.

It was you who drove me round England and Scotland; you who had the sole charge of my two horses throughout the 'caravan pilgrimage' described in these pages. It was you who related the story of our first adventures on the roads in your own book *The Brown Caravan*—which you dedicated to me.

So in return I can do no more than offer you the present volume. When you read it I hope you recall the happy times we spent together. I hope that you will see that I am not forgetful of your loyal service, or what would more truthfully be described as an ideal partnership.

My only regret is that unforseen obstacles made it impossible for you to tell the story of our subsequent adventures and experiences in the same breezy manner as you did in the previous book. You will note how much use I have made of your own journal; indeed certain chapters are based almost entirely on what you jotted down. Without having it for reference many incidents would have been forgotten, or related much less vividly—particularly all those portions of the book which deal with gipsies, tinkers, and such like folk we met on our journeys.

So please accept this record of our 'Rural Rides' through England and Scotland with the thanks and best wishes of your fellow 'caravan pilgrim.'

Yours ever,
P.F.A.

Macduff,
Banffshire.

Sept. 2nd, 1938.

FOREWORD

Mr. Peter Anson is much too well known both as a writer and artist to need any introduction from me. However, I gladly take this opportunity to pay a tribute to his work, which has been a delight to me in several volumes. *The Caravan Pilgrim* may prove to be the last account in English literature of such a journey. Horse-drawn caravans are still to be seen, but they are becoming as comparatively rare as full-rigged ships. The gipsies and tinkers have taken to second-hand motor cars, with good reason as Mr. Anson points out, now that the roads of Great Britain have been made petrol-minded. Mr. Anson wastes no time in sentimental regrets for the past, but throughout this long journey from Datchet, by the Thames, to the North-west of Scotland we are almost continuously aware of present obstacles to such leisurely progress. The particular object of the pilgrimage was to visit and record with that individual charm of draughtsmanship of which Mr. Anson possesses the secret, the various Catholic churches on that long road to the north. I found the account of the Yorkshire and Northumbrian parishes absorbing and the memories these parishes evoke of a long religious life which the Reformation could disturb but was unable to destroy, are poignant. It is bitter to reflect that what persecution could not effect is being effected now by the steady abolition of rural life in the supposed interest of our imperial mission. Squires, farmers, and labourers—they are all being gradually eradicated. And what is true of the rural districts in England where Catholicism has kept its hold is equally true of rural Scotland. No wonder Mr. Anson writes with a touch of bitterness about the obstruction of every attempt to start industries in the Highlands "by the sentimenal protests of wealthy landlords who complain that factory buildings, electric pylons, or workmen's cottages will ruin the ' amenities ' of the scenery." We have lately had an example of such ' sentimentality ' in the rejection by Parliament of the Lochaber Power Scheme. And of Banffshire, which is another stronghold of Catholicism, we hear that the Scottish herring industry is likely to pass soon into the hands of English companies. But the future of the fishing industry in Scotland is too melancholy a topic for an introduction, and it would be an injustice to Mr. Anson's book if I were to suggest that it was preoccupied with such themes. On the contrary it is as agreeable a piece of topography as one can wish to read, and to those who wish to learn something about England and Scotland from an unusual angle I warmly commend *The Caravan Pilgrim.* There are moments when the tarmac seems to have departed from the roads and when the scent of dust laid by a summer shower returns, moments of youth with the flowers and birds and hedges of long ago. How pleasant it is to turn the pages of a book in which Time himself is lenient!

COMPTON MACKENZIE.

CONTENTS

vii

LIST OF ILLUSTRATIONS

PREFACE

You will probably wonder why anybody in these days should wish to become the owner of a gipsy caravan and two horses and despite the obvious inconveniences and slowness of this antiquated method of travel, spend nearly twelve months wandering through the greater part of England and Scotland.

The reasons why I decided to adopt this vagrant life were purely practical ones. For several years I had been contributing a weekly series of drawings of Catholic churches to the *Universe*. This work involved constant travelling often for a long period at a stretch. The inconvenience of such a life became more and more obvious as time went on, until one day I suddenly made up my mind that I would have no more to do with hotels and railways, but would roam the countryside in my own home on wheels, and be quite independent of *Bradshaw* or the *ABC Railway Guide*.

Motors never appealed to me. Friends have always told me that I should never be able to drive a car. Speed was of no great importance. So I decided that I would buy a gipsy-caravan and rely on a horse instead of an internal combustion engine. But as I knew nothing about horses I had also to find a companion who could take charge of this department. I myself was quite prepared to look after the domestic side of the life, always enjoying cooking meals and doing house work.

Advertisements in two papers resulted in no less than two hundred applications for this job, incredible as it may seem. It took some time to sort out this flood of letters which poured in for several days. Finally I interviewed three of the would-be caravan drivers, and in the end engaged a man who, in addition to having a life-long experience of horses, was also a qualified blacksmith.

This young Yorkshireman from the Cleveland Hills has already put on record the story of our first two months on the road in *The Brown Caravan* (Heath Cranton, 1935). What an exciting two months they were! Far more so than the latter journeys which I have described in this book. For neither of us had ever lived in a caravan before, and knew nothing of the kind of difficulties which we should meet with. So we had to learn by experience, and very often we paid heavily for our ignorance.

When I bought my original caravan I did not consider the matter of weight. All I looked for was a comfortable and well-built wagon which would provide me with a reasonably spacious home on wheels. And I certainly got what I wanted. But after three days on the roads this mighty wagon proved to be too heavy for one horse to drag up more than a slight slope. Rather than leave it by the roadside and abandon my journey I was forced to purchase another horse. So ' Jack ' was provided with a companion whom we named ' Bill.' Even with two strong horses we often found ourselves in difficulties, and routes had to be chosen so as to avoid the worst hills. How many hours did I not spend poring over the Contour Road Book of England, studying gradients!

As I have related in these pages, when we reached the Yorkshire moors after a long and laborious journey from the Thames valley, it became clear that a lighter wagon was essential if we were to get round Scotland. I managed to find a smaller, although a far less luxurious, van which was our home for the rest of the year. The sacrifice of space and comfort was compensated for by the knowledge that henceforth we need fear no hills unless the gradients were more than 1 in 5.

I look back on that year's wandering through Great Britain as one of the happiest times in my life. The pleasure was derived not so much from seeing the country or from visiting certain places, for the route we covered was already familiar to me, if not to my companion, but in the chance meetings with all sorts of strange types of humanity—tramps, tinkers, gipsies, farmers, shopkeepers. Again there was the insight gained into the daily life of the Catholic church, for in almost every place in which we stopped for more than a day we were entertained by priests, monks, or nuns. I cannot name them individually, but if this book should come into their hands, I would like them to know that I have not forgotten their hospitality, nor all the trouble they took to find grazing for the two horses, which was always a problem.

I must likewise thank ' Jack ' and ' Bill ' for their share in the book, for with never a complaint, they pulled the caravan from the south of England to the north of Scotland and back again to Yorkshire, where to my great regret, I had to part with them. These two horses were the means of introduction to many people, for, thanks to the splendid condition in which they were kept by their driver, they never failed to arouse interest and admiration on the roads, or in the towns and villages through which we passed. Even today when motors have almost superseded horses as a means of transport, mankind still retains its love of a good horse.

Every year it becomes more and difficult to travel with horses. Even gipsies are being forced to take to motor cars. So I am glad I took this opportunity to experience of a way of travel which will soon be as obsolete as the sailing ship.

Perhaps I ought to apologise for having given so much space to detailed descriptions of churches, monasteries, and convents, which some readers may find rather boring. But many friends, who saw these drawings which originally appeared in the *Universe* have often asked if they could not be reprinted, and at the same time, if I could not tell them more about the actual journeys. It is with the permission of the editor of this paper that all these drawings illustrate the kindly lent for the purpose. My thanks are also due to the Abbot of Fort Augustus for the loan of the block on page 179.

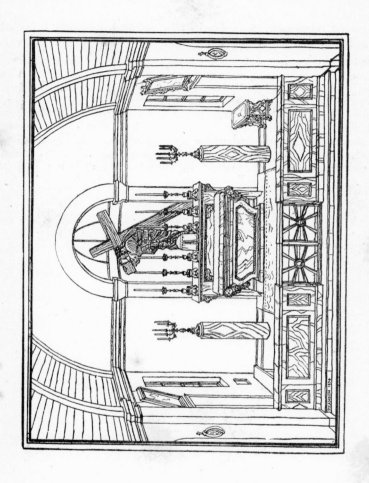

St. Augustine's, Datchet.

ONE

*Datchet—Watford—St. Albans—Welwyn Garden City—Ware
—St. Edmund's College.*

Just after nine o'clock we started on our pilgrimage with
black smudges on our foreheads. For it was Ash Wednesday.
So we are reminded that we are but dust and to dust we shall
return—if we meet with our last end on this pilgrimage. A
fitting send off to a journey from the Thames Valley to the
north of Scotland. We may be travelling for about six or nine
months, for it is uncertain just how long the horses will take
to cover the distance, and all sorts of unforseen accidents may
occur.

The caravan has been overhauled and repainted, both without and within. A new stove has been installed. Springs
and wheels have been oiled and tested. The two horses
have been exercised on the roads and in other ways, to get them
into training after a more or less idle three months. During
this time they had nothing to do but graze at leisure in a small
paddock belonging to the Canons Regular of the Lateran who
have charge of the little Baroque church at Datchet as well as
the Catholic church at Eton. The Canons also conduct
a secondary school for boys which may well claim to carry
on the main objects for which King Henry VI founded the
neighbouring college of Our Lady of Eton five centuries ago.
Both of these churches were built by the late Lord Braye;
himself an old Etonian, and the High Altar and other fittings
came from his private chapel at Stanford Hall, near Rugby.

We expected there would be some trouble when putting
Jack into the shafts. And we were not mistaken. He reared
up, just in his old way, and nearly broke some of the harness.
But Tony managed to hold him firm. His accompanying

3

remarks, not exactly polite, can be left to the imagination.

I led Bill out of the gate onto the road. The great lumbering caravan followed. Then Bill was put in to do his share of the job. We were off at last. Along the Eton road towards Datchet village. Here I called for groceries which had previously been ordered and made a few final purchases of other things forgotten at the last moment.

" Bruno "—the black cat—had been shut up in the van before starting. We did not want to leave him behind. Having been a house-cat since November he was terrified at the strange rocking movement of the wagon. Finding the door closed, he managed to climb out on the roof through one of the sky-lights. I was walking just behind the van. Suddenly I heard a plaintive " miaow " right above me. I looked up. In a flash the black kitten had jumped on to the road and was tearing back homewards. I gave chase and managed to capture the terrified animal. All I could do was to put him back in the van, hoping that he would soon get used to its motion. I shut the skylights as well as the door to make further escape impossible.

The sun was shining through a slight haze. There had been a frost in the night. The country still looked very wintry. Leaving Datchet we followed winding lanes northwards. Crossing the Bath Road, where the traffic needed careful negotiating, we made for Langley. Quite forgetting " Bruno," I opened the door of the caravan to consult a map. Out jumped the cat, and disappeared behind some cottages. We waited nearly twenty minutes, hoping that he would return. But we waited in vain. Despairing of ever seeing him again, and hoping that he would find a new home, we decided to move on. It seemed that Bruno was more fitted for a domestic than a gipsy life.

Owing to the hold up at Langley a good half hour had been wasted, so there was no time to call on the Bridgettine nuns at Iver Heath, as I had intended. I wanted to reach St. Albans before dusk, if possible. So we moved on northwards.

4

We stopped for dinner just beyond the film studios at Denham. The horses needed a rest, although the roads we had traversed had been almost dead level. They were not yet pulling together easily. About six miles further on we halted again—outside the church of Our Lady Help of Christians, just beyond Rickmansworth. There was a good deal of traffic on the road, especially when passing through Watford, and care was needed to negotiate it. Here I paid a hurried visit to the Church of the Holy Rood; designed by J. F. Bentley, the architect of Westminster Cathedral. The latter is his most famous work, but Watford is far more characteristic of his genius. For Bentley had an essentially " Gothic " mind. Here, thanks to the generosity of the donor, he had a free hand to indulge in his passion for elaborate detail and ornament. The result is one of the most ornately decorated Catholic churches to be built in England since the Reformation.

The afternoon seemed to pass very quickly. By the time we had got through Watford it was already growing dusk, and a damp mist was rising. I realised it was impossible to reach St. Albans that night. I began to look out for a camp site. About four miles on we stopped at the " Black Boy " Inn. Here I asked if there was a field in which our horses could graze. Unlike so many other subsequent occasions, I was lucky the first time. I was told that the field exactly opposite the inn was at our disposal. I opened the gate and Tony drove in. The horses were let loose, and within half an hour we ourselves were enjoying our tea within the cosy interior of the van ; the red curtains drawn across the windows, and the little stove giving out a welcome heat. It froze hard that night, but we were very snug.

The following morning we were on the road again after an early breakfast. Two hours later we reached St. Albans. Here both caravan, horses and drivers were photographed. The picture was a success (*see frontispiece*). It appeared in the next issue of the *Universe* with the following caption :

" **Our pilgrim artist on the road coaxes his horses up Holy-**

well Hill, along a highway which long ago was crowded with pilgrims to the shrine of St. Alban."

The reporter went on to inform readers that "Mr. Anson, after a day's sketching under the shade of the old abbey, hitched up his horses to his caravan, and took the open road again . . . to follow (but more leisurely) Dick Turpin to York."

I am afraid this 'blurb' was not quite true to facts, for I never went near the ' shade of the old abbey '—the only sketch I made being of the not very attractive modern Catholic Church which makes no attempt to rival the ancient Benedictine abbey either in style or decoration.

Thanks to the *Universe* staff, for this great Catholic weekly is printed in St. Albans, we have got an excellent camp site within a mile of the city. To-night I am writing in the caravan, which is standing in the yard of an empty farm. Jack and Bill are able to graze in perfect freedom, for they have sole possession of its paddocks.

To-day we have covered the distance between St. Albans and St. Edmund's College, Old Hall Green, a mile or two south of Buntingford. We made an early start, stopping for breakfast about 9 o'clock just before entering Welwyn Garden City.

This modern township seemed to be a perfect maze of roads, and we got lost. There was a mist hanging over the country-side and it was almost impossible to get our bearings. With no sun to guide one it is difficult to tell the points of the compass. Tony has not much sense of direction and can never understand how I can tell which is the north or south. It is a perpetual mystery to him! I suppose that farmers, unlike sailors, do not have to trouble their heads about latitude and longitude; their job lying within a certain definite area?

But the familiar white-washed buildings of the Shredded Wheat Factory which I had often seen from the L.N.E.R. main line served as a beacon, and after a good deal of wandering about we regained the main road once more. Nothing of any interest or excitement happened, as we rumbled on mile after

6

mile, each of us taking a spell with the reins. We passed through Hertford and Ware. Then we turned north along the road well known to motorists as A.14.

On reaching the top of a steep descent before Wadesmill I noticed an even steeper hill on the other side of the valley. I wondered if it would prove to be beyond the pulling powers of the horses. Putting on the heavy cross shoe to the left back-wheel, Tony led Jack down the hill. I followed with Bill. Having got to the bottom I told my companion to stop, while I went on ahead to see what the road surface and gradients were like. It seemed a very long and steep climb. There was nothing to be done but boldly face it. So putting the horses in single traces we started off. Every moment we expected the horses would stop. If they had done so it would have been impossible to make a fresh start. I walked close behind the van, ready to shove in the wooden block to prevent the van slipping back, should the worst come to the worst. But somehow or other we managed to reach the top. Here we had a rest, before moving on again.

Motorists will find it difficult to realise why we should have had all this bother. They would not even have to change gears. But a great lumbering gipsy caravan drawn by two horses is a different proposition!

About four miles beyond we came in sight of the roofs of St. Edmund's College rising up above trees. Half an hour later the caravan was parked in one of the playing fields, opposite the oldest portion of the college buildings. Jack and Bill were grazing in a more distant paddock while the Rector, Mgr. Bickford, was showing us round the vast establishment of which he has charge.

Only a small portion of the various scattered groups of buildings which to-day make up St. Edmund's College were standing when the first batch of students were brought here by Bishop Douglass on their arrival in England in 1793 after their expulsion from Douai at the time of the French Revolution. The seminary at Douai was founded by Cardinal Allen in 1568.

7

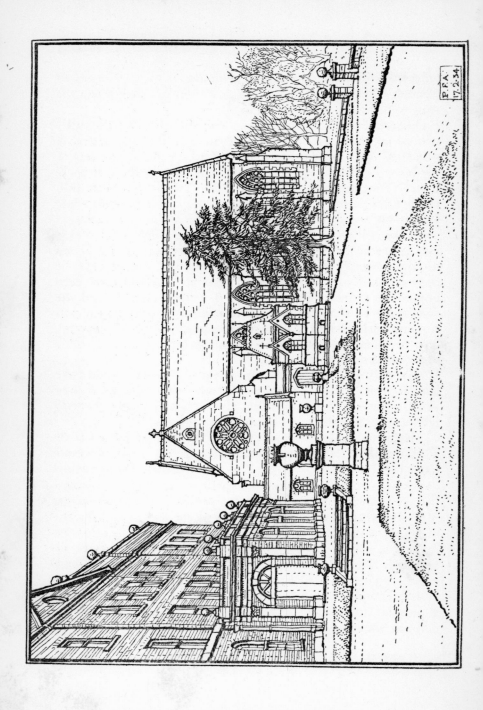

St. Edmund's College, Old Hall, Ware.

But from the first St. Edmund's College combined two distinct establishments for in addition to the seminary there was a school for lay boys, originally established at Twyford in 1695. To-day after nearly 150 years of expansion and development St. Edmund's still retains its dual character. It is now a seminary for the archdiocese of Westminster and a flourishing school for lay boys.

Nothing could have exceeded the kind welcome given us by the Rector and professors. Tony and myself dined in the refectory, feeling conscious of the honour paid to us by being invited to sit at the High Table, where we could look down on the crowd of seminarists.

We assisted at High Mass from the Rood Loft of Augustus Welby Pugin's graceful Gothic chapel. The unaccompanied singing was a pleasure to hear, and the ceremonies a model of quiet dignity and precision.

We were shown the great library, the historical portraits and the tombs of the Vicars Apostolic of the London District. St. Edmund's College as it exists to-day is a visible memorial to the late Cardinal Bourne, who completely reorganised the whole establishment, as well as adding to the buildings. He himself, in accordance with his wishes, is buried in the Galilee Chapel, erected by himself.

We talked to a number of the students, and during that Sunday afternoon had relays of them wanting to have a peep inside the caravan.

TWO

*Buntingford—Baldock—Shefford—the Great North Road
—Blackfriars School, Laxton.*

We have been two days on the road since leaving St.
Edmund's College. Tony's younger brother, a Canon Regular
of the Lateran, who with other students motors over here from
his monastery at Hoddesdon to attend lectures in theology,
came with us as far as the college gates.

Having said good-bye to him we proceeded along the main
road through Puckeridge to Buntingford, a typical old Hertfordshire town, with a Gothic church, erected as a memorial
to the late Mgr. Robert Hugh Benson, who died at Salford in
October, 1914. Mgr. Benson is buried in the chapel erected
in the garden of his picturesque Queen Anne house at Hare
Street where most of his later novels were written. Here he
used to retire for a brief rest between his exhausting labours
of missionary activity.

Between Buntingford and Baldock we passed through on
over a rolling countryside of chalk hills. It was a pleasant
surprise to discover that it is as yet completely unspoilt by
housing estates. So far it appears to have escaped the notice
of the speculative builder of bungalows. It is difficult to
realise one is within less than twenty-five miles of London.
Nearly all this corner of Hertfordshire is well farmed. For
this reason we failed to discover any likely spot to camp
until we were past Baldock. At last, as it was growing dusk,
we stopped in the little village of Rodwell, just off the Great
North Road. Here a farmer made us very welcome. Butter,
milk and eggs were for sale, and feeling very hungry we sat
down to a good square meal.

10

P.F.A. 1934.

St. Francis', Shefford.

We started off again, after breakfast, reaching Shefford about midday. Here, right in the heart of this sleepy old town, is St. Francis' Home, an orphanage for boys. The rector, Fr. Wilson, to whom I had written to announce our arrival, welcomed us very hospitably. Tony was pleased to discover a fellow Yorkshireman; in itself more than sufficient introduction. The caravan is parked in a marshy playing field where we hope the wheels will not sink too deep in the soft ground to make it impossible to get away.

The orphan boys are housed in a rambling group of red brick buildings, adjoining which is a small, but extremely ornate Gothic church, erected by the late Mrs. Lyne-Stephens, who also built the Catholic church of the English Martyrs at Cambridge.

The boys seem to be a very cheerful and happy family. There is nothing of the ' institutional ' atmosphere about St. Francis Home. The highest compliment one can pay is to say that it is Franciscan not only in name but in spirit.

Needless to say the boys are very curious to visit the caravan. More than one of these friendly little lads says how much he would like to join us on our long journey to the far north of Scotland. And what normal boy would not jump at such a chance to ' see the world '?

I am writing up my notes sitting in the caravan which is standing in the centre of the courtyard of what used to be the stables of a big classical mansion known as Laxton Hall, situated in the north-west corner of Northamptonshire. To-day Laxton Hall has become Blackfriars School, under the charge of the Dominican Fathers. The stables are no longer occupied by carriages and hunters, but are devoted to more mercenary and less aristocratic purposes as befits a boys' school.

We had a great send off at Shefford; the orphan boys gathering to watch the caravan's departure. I can well believe that our visit will not be quickly forgotten.

Mile after mile we rumbled on, having rejoined the Great

12

North Road at Sandy. The country was somewhat monotonous. Brussels sprouts, cabbages and potatoes are good to eat in moderation, but one can get rather bored when forced to gaze at endless flat fields of nothing else for a whole morning, especially when owing to the absence of sun and a dull grey sky, there are no contrasts of light and shade.

The Great North Road was so busy, and the stream of traffic so continuous, that careful driving was necessary. Every few minutes great big lorries would roar past us; their drivers giving us glances of mingled surprise and amusement. Sometimes on going through a village men would stop and ask us where we were bound for, having expressed their admiration at the well-groomed and well-conditioned horses.

After a week on the roads Jack and Bill are now working well together. But Bill has a tiresome trick of keeping his leather traces half taut when we are mounting a slight rise. If Tony isn't watching, Bill will lag behind and then the traces slacken. There were times when this laziness rouses my companion to an outburst of good honest cursing to relieve his pent up feelings. But Bill isn't really lazy. He's just cute. Jack, on the contrary, can, and will pull his head off for all Bill cares and the van keeps rolling. At first Bill used to crawl along so slowly that quite often he would get a dig on his hind quarters from the van! But now he has developed a new trick or two, which involves a constant stirring on from the driver. " Come on Bill! " is Tony's perpetual exclamation. Still he is a good caravan horse. He is even tempered, rather stolid, with a sly twinkle in his eye occasionally. One is always sure of him no matter what chains or harness he is in.

Jack is a completely different type of horse, full of character and spirit. He is certainly Tony's favourite. He is never tired of praising his good points. Both Jack and Bill have still got their winter coats on them, having never been under cover even during snow. So they are both very strong and hardy. No wonder men stop and look at them, for it isn't often that such horses—and such a caravan—are seen on the roads in these

13

days. When we tell people that we are bound for Scotland they stare in amazement, as if unable to realise how we shall get there. "You've a long way to go yet" is a favourite remark. So we drive on leaving the men to gossip about us as they drink their pints of beer in the public houses.

About six o'clock we arrived at a peaceful little village named Alconbury Western in Huntingdonshire. Here, after several enquiries, I managed to find a field for the horses, into which we drove, and where the caravan rested for the night. After supper Tony gathered 'local colour' while conversing with the natives in one of the village 'pubs.' I myself wrote letters and then went to bed.

We were up very early, in fact before sunrise. There had been frost during the night and the ground was quite white. As was so often the case Jack and Bill had gone off to the most remote corner of their field, and could only be caught with the aid of much whistling and a basin of corn held out to lure them from afar. The Great North Road was almost deserted, but a few big motor lorries which had been driving all night, sped past us as we rumbled on at our usual four miles an hour. On this stretch the Great North Road follows the old Roman Ermine Street, which has scarcely a bend on it for many a mile. We stopped for lunch near Wansford, one of the most beautiful of the stone-built Northamptonshire villages. Its ancient bridge is perhaps more picturesque than safe. But a new by-pass has been made with a modern concrete bridge across the river Welland.

Leaving Wansford we turned left climbing up a long hill, and across a lonely bit of country where the fields are divided by stone walls, or 'dykes' as they are called in the north of England and Scotland. Then we descended another long hill into the valley of the Welland.

As the sun was setting we drew up at the entrance of a winding drive, whose surface was in urgent need of repair. At length the grey stone mansion of Laxton Hall came into view.

14

The Headmaster, Fr. Henry St. John, O.P., was at the door to welcome us. As I have already stated the caravan was driven into the stables; Jack and Bill being set free to wander as they chose in the park. Here they made friends with a mare. In fact Jack most definitely ' got off ' with her.

During the night the pair of them managed to find their way into the vegetable garden, leaving Bill, always less intelligent than his companion, to munch grass. Not until the morning did I hear that two of the Fathers had been obliged to rise from their beds about 2 a.m., and prevent Jack and his lady-friend from stealing yet more " forbidden fruit " for they had already managed to eat a lot of lettuces. It was a case of the Garden of Eden over again!

There can be few Catholic schools in England which equal Laxton for charm of situation. The stately 18th century mansion is surrounded by a large park on the borders of a forest.

Founded at Bornhem in Flanders as long ago as 1660; re-established at Hinckley in Leicestershire in 1826; the school was removed to Hawksyard, near Lichfield, in 1898. Here it grew and prospered, with the result that the Dominican Fathers had to find larger quarters for the boys after twenty-five years.

There is a happy ' family ' atmosphere at Laxton. In spite of being fully occupied in teaching, the Fathers manage to find time for prayer as well as an active apostolate. They carry out the usual round of liturgical offices in their temporary chapel, which cannot be described as beautiful or convenient. It was a pleasure to hear the perfectly sung plain chant at High Mass, and to end each day with the Dominican ' Salve Regina ' after Compline in which the boys' voices alternated with those of the community.

May it not be long before Blackfriars School has a more worthy and dignified chapel—the only feature which seemed out of keeping with the place.

Blackfriars School, Laxton.

THREE

Stamford—The Fens—Spalding—Boston—Horncastle —Panton College.

After three days at Laxton we set off again on our journey northwards. Our road led through Stamford, that lovely old town, where my companion, in spite of little interest in architecture, became enthusiastic over the stone-built houses and stately churches. Here I made a sketch of the modern Catholic church, erected in 1845 when the surrounding countryside was suddenly invaded by an army of Irish agricultural labourers, driven from their native land as the result of the potato famine. And so, as in many other places, the Old Religion was brought back to Stamford after an interval of nearly three centuries.

Leaving Stamford on this bright spring-like morning, with an east wind drying up the roads, still muddy after last night's heavy rain, we found ourselves on the last bit of rising ground above the Fens.

We stopped for lunch where there was a view over miles of country, as level as a table. Then crossing the L.N.E.R. main line at Tallington, we came to the straggling villages of West Deeping, Market Deeping, and Deeping Gate. Here I shouted to Tony to turn left where there was a signpost marked ' Spalding.'

The Fens can become very monotonous when rumbling over them in a slow moving caravan at four miles an hour. This is what we both agreed on that February afternoon. Flat fields, broken up with long 'dykes' of stagnant water, are the regular and unchanging features of the landscape. In summer these

17

Our Lady and St. Augustine, Stamford.

fields are gay with a variety of colour. But in February they are mostly sombre black, for the soil is almost as dark as a peat bog.

It wasn't so dull for the first few hours. In fact we rather enjoyed the pleasant idleness, with nothing to do but keep the reins slack, with no anxiety or bother about ' banks,' as my Yorkshire companion always describes any kind of gradient. We watch the men and horses working together for a common end. We glance at the windmills or the distant towers of village churches which stand up like landmarks to guide the traveller across the Fens.

Tony says that he is getting ' fed up ' with the flatness. He allows me to drive more than usual, partly because he knows I can't come to any harm, also because, as he remarks " When I'm walking I can't see so far as when perched up on that seat." I tell him that artists often come here in summer to paint the Fen country. " Well! " says he, " I can't see what there is to paint, except the sky." " That's right," I explain. " The artists choose the Fens just because of it's unbroken skies." " Who wants to look at a picture of clouds, I'd like to know," was his disgusted comment. " How much longer shall we be before we get out of this country? " I reply that I hope we shall be well away from the fens by to-morrow evening when we ought to be climbing the Lincolnshire Wolds.

" We'll stop at the first field we can find. Take the reins while I go and try my luck at this next farm. Wait until I come back."

So getting down off the van I walked on ahead to the farm ; the first sign of human habitation we had sighted for nearly two miles. Tony gave the horses a feed of corn, then disappeared within the van to warm himself at the stove.

The weather had changed during the past two hours and had become very cold. The pale wintry sun had disappeared behind dark grey clouds. The wind had shifted to the north east, and was blowing with a razor-like keeness.

I was unsuccessful in my search for a field in which the horses could graze. The farmer stared suspiciously at the van in the distance. Evidently he didn't like the look of us. He informed me quite positively that he had cattle in every field—although as a matter of fact my own eyes disproved the exact truth of this statement. He suggested I should try the next farm.

So I returned to the van. On hearing that I had been unlucky, Tony remarked with a sarcastic smile, "Oh! I see. Any excuse is better than none. On a cold night like this all the cows and stock will be inside. It's clear enough that the man didn't want us. Come on, Peter, we'd better be moving."

We set off again. I tried three other farms with no better result. Next I called at a small wayside 'pub.' But there was 'nothing doing' and the innkeeper could only advise me to make for Spalding.

By this time it was nearly dark. Tony lit the lamps and while he was doing this, snow began to fall. Within a quarter of an hour the road was white. The wind was against us, and with the snow blowing into his eyes, Tony found it difficult to see where he was driving. The tired horses stumbled on wearily; the van sounding strangely silent as its wheels moved over the soft carpet of snow. I kept a good look out for any light, in the hope that we might soon reach another farm, when the owner would scarcely turn us away on such a night as this. There was nothing else to do but struggle on through the snow, for the horses couldn't be let loose, even if the van had been backed into the side of the road.

Suddenly I caught sight of a dark shape in a field below the road—for all the roads hereabouts are on a higher level than the fields. As we came nearer I realised that it was a caravan. Then I noticed a dim light burning within.

"Stop!" I shouted to Tony. "Look! There's a gipsy-wagon!"

I clambered over a gate, and floundered through the snow. Mounting the steps of the van I knocked at the door.

It was opened by a typical looking gipsy. In the background was a woman. A smell of fried bacon greeted me. The man and the woman were at tea.

I explained our plight—that our own caravan was in the road, and that we had been unable to find anywhere to spend the night. Could the gipsy advise me what to do? Could we get our van into this same field?

He was doubtful as the snow had begun to drift, and the van might get struck fast or even topple over if we tried to shift it from the road down the steep bank into the field.

"We van-dwellers must help each other," says he with a smile, showing his white teeth. "I reckon I'd better take you along to the farmer who owns this field. Maybe he'd let you leave your van in the lane and give you a stable for the horses. You can't leave 'em out on a night like this. Come far to-day?"

"From beyond Stamford," I told him.

He put on his cap and tying a muffler round his neck, followed me across the snow to the road, where our caravan was still waiting.

"That's a heavy waggon you've got there. We'd never be able to shift it in the snow."

The gipsy was right—it would have been impossible. He greeted Tony in a friendly manner, and directed him to turn down a lane alongside the broad dyke.

In about five minutes we came to a low group of farm buildings. The gipsy led me to the back door which was opened by the farmer himself. When he heard my story of how all the other farmers had been unable to give us a field and had turned us away, he said at once that the van could be parked in the lane, and insisted that Jack and Bill must occupy an empty stable. He helped Tony and the gipsy to unloose them and led them away into the yard.

21

I myself retired to the van and made hurried preparations for a long overdue meal. For it was now getting on for eight o'clock and both Tony and myself were cold, tired, and hungry. That 'high tea' was one of the most welcome meals I can remember during all our journeys. Never were fried bacon and eggs eaten with such relish. After tea Tony went off in the snow to visit our gipsy neighbours in their caravan. I decided it was preferable to stay indoors.

When he returned at a late hour I had been in bed at least an hour. It seemed that he had spent an interesting and profitable time. He lit the lamp, and was so eager to relate all he had heard and seen, that I had to rouse myself to listen.

This was our first contact with real gipsies. From now onwards we regarded them as friends whose acquaintance was to be sought for, not to be avoided.

John Smith and his wife—for such was the man's name—had travelled south from Doncaster, so Tony informed me. What is more, they looked upon themselves as distinctly superior, for were they not closely related to Gipsy Smith, the famous evangelist? At one time John Smith, so he told my companion, had been prosperous enough to own three fine horses and an even bigger van than ours—one of those palatial wagons adorned with carving, and an interior brilliantly decorated with polished mahogany, gleaming brass, and innumerable mirrors. But owing to bad luck both horses and van had been sold. To-day they had to make-do with a ramshackle old waggon and a sorry-looking nag. We could quite understand why they envied us. In fact the man, like every gipsy, always ready for a business deal, had suggested to Tony that as we had such a long journey before us, it would be much to _our_ advantage to 'swop' vans—and let him have one of our horses in addition. He pointed out, not without truth, that a light van would be able to climb any hill, and that one horse to feed would cost half two horses. But at the moment I did not feel inclined to accept the offer. Later on, as will be related, I realised he was right.

Tony then produced from his pocket a dirty crumpled bit of paper. " Look here," he said, " he's given me a list of places where we shall be welcome if we tell the folk that John Smith has sent us along. He says they don't charge much either."

I examined the document with curiosity. There were various farms, the names of inns and ' pubs' in towns and villages— a list of ' recommended houses' which we found far more useful to us than the addresses given in the ' Camping Club's' Handbook, which seldom catered for horses, only motor-caravans and trailers. It seemed that we had now been initiated into the brotherhood of the roads and could now regard ourselves as real vagrants, who were allowed to avail themselves of advantages and privileges only known to those who were in the business.

This dirty slip of paper reminded me that, during the 18th and early 19th centuries, the gipsy chiefs were in the habit of giving tokens or passes to those who had befriended them in any way. These tokens afforded a complete protection to the bearer if he were ever molested by gipsies, but were only 'valid' within the district in which they had been issued. Mr. Walter Simson in his *History of the Gipsies,* published in 1865, tells us that these passes were usually made of tin, with certain characters marked on them each tribe having its own special marking. On the other hand a token issued by the Baillie tribe of gipsies protected the bearer throughout Scotland. Trades-men in some districts where gipsies were very numerous would not venture far from home without tokens or passes. Mr. Simson informs us that the butchers and shoemakers of Lin-lithgow always travelled with tokens to prevent themselves being robbed, so too the pedlers throughout the Scottish Low-lands. Sometimes pen-knives were given instead of the usual tin tokens, and often saved the lives as well as the property of the bearers.

The sun was shining brightly when we woke up next morning. When I looked out of the window the ground was still white with snow; the sky was blue and cloudless. An early start was impossible; we must wait until the snow had thawed.

During the forenoon we had further talks with the gipsies, with whom Tony was now on intimate terms, due to a common knowledge of horseflesh and the fact that both he and they regarded Yorkshire as the finest county in England. As for ' southerners,' i.e., everyone who had the misfortune to be born south of the Humber or Mersey—as a race they were a poor lot; a hard-fisted, money-grabbing set of scoundrels.

"The southerners treat us like dirt," said John Smith. "Farmers think you want to buy their land by the price they ask for a night. Let 'em keep their money. Still we make a bit all the same. That bitch is a real meat getter. She'll snap up anything with fur on it. She's found us many a good meal."

I was anxious to give the gipsies something in return for having come to our aid. Money would have been regarded as an insult. However a few tactful questions produced the statement that any old clothes would be welcome. I looked through the cupboards, and decided that I could spare a pair of much worn trousers and two shirts. John Smith changed into them at once, strutting about quite proudly with his hands deep in the pockets.

By midday the sun had melted the snow enough to allow us to set off. We took Jack and Bill from the warm stable where they had passed the night in unaccustomed luxury, and soon had them harnessed.

After paying the farmer and buying milk, butter, and eggs; a final handshake with the gipsy and his wife, we drove away northwards. I looked back as the road turned and the latter were still waving to us.

Tony wanted to know something about the history of the gipsy race, and how they came to adopt their present way of

life. Maybe some of my readers may be interested to have a
few facts concerning this people who, in spite of every effort
to suppress them, still manage to continue to live in much the
same way as they have done since they first came into Europe
about eight hundred years ago. Where they actually came
from in the first instance has never been discovered, and
historians still continue to argue and disagree among themselves. All that is certain is that the Gipsies crossed the
Bosphorus and entered Europe in the early years of the 14th
century. On the other hand, in contradiction to this theory,
there are evidences of another migration of a similar Asiatic
race into Europe during the 11th or 12th century, who may or
may not have been of gipsy origin. But whoever they were,
their way of life differed very little from that of their present-
day descendants as can be proved from a rhymed paraphrase of
the Book of Genesis, written about 1120, in which the writer
describes the " Ishmaelitish folk " (supposed to be descended
from the son of Hagar), who have " neither house nor country ;
every place is the same to them. They roam about the land,
and abuse the people by their knaveries. It is thus that they
deceive folk, robbing no one openly." But again, there are
proofs of yet an earlier migration of a race of eastern origin
into central and western Europe long before this. They carried
on the trade of tinsmiths and ironworkers. One hears of them
at Constantinople in the 11th century; dwelling in little oblong
black tents, like those of the Arabs. After the entry into
Europe of the race now known as gipsies in the 14th century,
they gradually spread themselves throughout the Balkans ; then
moved into Hungary, and so across Germany, until they reached
Paris in 1427. About 1500 the first gipsies landed in England.
Five years later we hear of them in Scotland. They represented
themselves as Egyptian pilgrims, and won the sympathy and
support of James IV, who gave their chief—one Antonius
Gawino, the Earl of Little Egypt (said to be " pilgriming over
the Christian world by command of the Pope ")—a letter of
recommendation to the King of Denmark. Gipsies have never

shown any sign of having any definite religion of their own other than certain superstitions.

One of the most curious characteristics of the medieval gipsies, and indeed those of later times, was the habit of conforming to the particular religion of any country in which they made their home, at least so far as externals were concerned. There can be little doubt that this plea that they were under the Pope's protection was purely fictitious, and merely invented by themselves as a sure means of obtaining the support of ecclesiastics and credulous layfolk! Anyhow, so astute were these first gipsies both in England and in Scotland, that they were not only tolerated but even encouraged. But within less than ten years they had ceased to impose on the English, and in 1549 we hear of measures being enacted against them owing to the robberies and other crimes they committed. James V of Scotland seems to have been quite won over to the fascinating charm of these visitors to his kingdom. He went so far as to make a league of treaty with John Faw, Lord and Earl of Little Egypt, which granted innumerable privileges to himself and his followers so long as they lived peaceably and observed the laws of the kingdom of Scotland. From a purely legal aspect this curious document would seem to be nothing else than a clever excuse on the part of the gipsies to enable them to remain in Scotland now that their supposed 'pilgrimage' was ended! But the following year after the king himself had been molested by a band of gipsies when he travelled through Fife in disguise, and treated very roughly by them, for they thought he was a spy, he ordered all gipsies to leave Scotland. James V died soon after this decree, and so the gipsies were allowed to remain—wandering up and down the land without any measures being taken to control their movements until 1579, after which date many laws were passed to suppress them.

In the reign of Queen Elizabeth it was estimated that there were at least 10,000 gipsies roaming about England. She forbade her subjects to consort with them, and if this was discovered it was to be tried as an act of felony. Many unfortunate persons were executed merely because they were gipsies —the last gipsy to incur the death penalty for this reason have been condemned in the reign of Charles II. The English gipsies have always been more a race apart than those in Scotland, who in spite of frequent efforts to keep them in check, have again and again taken their place as equals with noble families, often priding themselves of being the bastard children of the lairds, which considering the license which was tolerated in past centuries, is not improbable. In England gipsies were frequently brought to trial on the charge of sorcery and witchcraft, and even worse crimes, for which there would seem to be little evidence.

The persecution of gipsies was not confined to Great Britain. Even worse treatment was meted out to them in Germany, Hungary, Spain, and Rumania at certain periods. No matter in what part of Europe one goes, the physical appearance of the gipsies, and as well as their manner of life is more or less identical. But the modern gipsy, in England and Scotland, whether male or female, lacks the picturesqueness of a former generation, although there still persists that passionate love of bright colour in details of clothing, and even a certain cut of clothes. Nearly every gipsy we met on our travels, and they numbered a good few after twelve months on the roads, revealed himself as an artist, even if his powers of self-expression were far less developed as those of a Spanish *Gitano* or Hungarian *Tzigany*, for we have no gipsy music in this country which can be compared with that of certain foreign lands.

The English gipsies seem to express their artistic instincts more in colour than in music, as witnessed by the care which is bestowed on the decoration of their wagons, some of which are real works of art. It is not generally realised that the typical gipsy caravan—such as that which was our own home—is of comparatively recent introduction, and not found in many other countries. Until quite late on in the last century English gipsies lived in tents, and travelled about the country with horses and asses. Sometimes they had small carts, but not always. Caravans have never gained the same popularity with Scottish gipsies as English ones, and even to-day the average Scottish 'tinker' (as gipsies are usually termed) is content to roam about with horses and tents, the latter of almost exactly the same shape and construction as was used by the first gipsies who came into Europe more than eight centuries ago. In many instances horses have been discarded in favour of an antiquated motor-car which looks as if it had been picked up off a scrap heap of old iron! But even if this more modern method of transport has been adopted, and with good reason, for petrol costs less than the upkeep of a horse, and an old car can be bought for about half the price of a horse, the manner of life remains almost unchanged, as will be shown in a later chapter where I shall have more to say about Scottish tinkers.

If one wants to see some fine specimens of really ' de luxe gipsy caravans of the old type, they can still be discovered in some of those large encampments round London, for instance on the Belvedere Marshes, a few miles east of Woolwich; or at Hounslow and Mitcham—to name but a few places which I have visited myself. Some of these wagons may have cost as much as £500, and I was told that our own van, which was not nearly so ornate as some of them, certainly cost at least £250 in the first instance. The painting and decoration of the interior is in itself a costly process as I learnt from experience. Just before setting out on this journey to Yorkshire I wanted to have the van repainted. I was given the address of a gipsy caravan painter near Hounslow, who when he had examined the van, told me that he could not possibly do the job for less than £35, and what is more, he maintained that it would lower his artistic reputation if he attempted to do it in a manner which was not up to his normal standard! I pleaded with him that I did not want any elaborate scroll work or lining, but to no purpose. He pointed out to me that he was a professional artist as well as myself, and asked me if I would do a job for

28

anybody if they wanted me to do less than my best?   He explained that a good wagon like ours demanded nothing but the best work, that it would be almost sacrilege to deny it the marvellous elaboration of detail on the body, wheels and under-carriage, which badly needed renewing.   In the end, when I told him quite frankly that I could not afford £35 at that moment, he suggested that I should buy some orange and white striped canvas with which to drape the sides of the van, so as to make people believe that it was to protect its paintwork from the sun, instead of merely to hide its blisters and lack of varnish!   " Come back again next winter " were his parting words of advice.   " I dare say you may be able to afford the money by then, and I'll be glad to do the job for you."

In spite of all the many learned treatises which have been written on them, the origin of the gipsies still remain more or less a mystery, and they themselves continue to be a race apart from the rest of mankind, far more so than the Jews. Among themselves the real gipsies—for there are many who are no more than half-breeds—still retain their own Romany tongue, although much corrupted through the introduction of alien words and phrases. I have been told that the difference between the Romany which is spoken in Eastern Europe and in England is so great that only with difficulty would a Hungarian gipsy be able to converse with an English one.   Philologists would seem to be more or less agreed, so it would appear, that Romany must be derived from some Indian dialect, although it contains a large number of Greek and Persian words, not to mention those of other languages of people among whom the gipsies have dwelt for a certain period of their migrations.

The more one lives among gipsies and talks with them, the more one sympathises with the difficulty they have to retain their independence, for measures are being imposed, and which grow more and more difficult to evade, to suppress 'vagrancy,' which in itself is regarded as a crime—a state of life contrary to the ideals of ' modern civilisation.'   One wonders how long the gipsies in England and Scotland will be able to fight against

29

laws which render their manner of living almost impossible. From my own experience of twelve months as an amateur ' vagrant ' I realised that the obstacles against living such a life are overwhelming. The increase of cheap multiple-stores in almost every town spells ruin to gipsies, for they are thus deprived of the market for their goods which has been their chief means of livelihood for centuries. In the face of mass-produced machine-made tin-ware, earthen-ware, and other house-hold articles, formerly made by gipsies themselves, how can they compete with such rivals? The days of hawkers, tinkers, knife-grinders, basket-weavers, broom makers, and such-like craftsmen, would seem to be numbered. Horse dealing too is rapidly becoming almost a ' luxury trade,' for horses are no longer a necessity to mankind, but merely a means of pleasure for those who can afford to keep them for sport. So what is left to the gipsies, and how can they adjust themselves to a generally standardised way of living which is to be found in all classes of society? The moral persecution which they now have to endure is more likely to exterminate them as a race than were the purely physical tortures and persecutions of past ages. It is killing the soul of the gipsy, not merely his body.

Such were my thoughts that morning in February as we moved along across the Fens, after our long talks with the gipsy and his wife. This rather pathetic couple seemed to sum up in themselves the degradation of a what was once a magnificent race, proud and self-sufficient. One could still detect traces of a noble ancestry, even beneath the sordid exterior of this man and woman. The spirit was not yet quenched, but life had become almost too hard for them. Given the right environment they might yet be capable of reverting to what their ancestors must have been. But how little is left to them, and what chances have they? All the old trades by which they could formerly earn their living are slipping from their grasp. Horse dealing is no longer profitable—even poaching is hardly

Our Lady and St. Norbert, Spalding.

worth while, so strict are the laws, so wary the police! So these two vagabonds have nothing else to do but struggle on against a stream whose force they are unable to resist, and which in the long run, will probably drag them down lower and lower until they become open criminals in sheer self-defence. And then what will be their fate?

But my meditations were cut short by the realisation that we had now arrived at Spalding and that I had to buy some groceries since the larder was empty, also that Tony needed some corn for his horses. We discovered it was a market-day, and the streets were so crowded that it was sometime before we found a quiet place to 'park' the caravan.

The Catholic religion was completely unrooted in this district, and not until 1876 did it regain a foothold in Spalding when the Premonstratensian Canons built a small church in the town, chiefly for the need of the Irish agricultural workers. In pre-Reformation times this same Order had charge of no less than thirty parishes in Lincolnshire. After many enquiries I found the modern Catholic church, hidden away in a back street. To my surprise there was a realistic Lourdes grotto, which, from the numerous ' ex voto ' tablets put up around it, seems to be quite frequented by pilgrims, whose prayers have been answered here.

From Spalding to Boston is a country of the same kind as we had passed through yesterday, but with more trees, well set with fine churches. This proves that it must have been equally productive land before the Reformation.

That afternoon we did not get further than the village of Sutterton. Here we were told by an innkeeper that we could park the caravan in the back yard, and that he had a good field for the horses. We were fortunate. Within half an hour of having got fixed up, snow began to fall again, and it continued all night.

When we woke up this morning we realised that it was useless to think of making a move. There was at least four to six inches of snow in the inn yard, and we are prisoners until it shall choose to thaw. A ' Fried Fish and Chips ' van also sought shelter in the yard, and from its interior comes forth appetising smells. I have sampled its fare, and find both fish and chips so good that I bought enough to provide us with dinner and supper to-day.

With nothing else to do I have spent the whole afternoon in writing up the events of the past forty-eight hours.

The morning after I wrote the last paragraph the snow had melted on the tar-mac road, at least sufficiently to allow us to get away from the inn yard where we had spent some thirty-six hours. The remains of the fish and chips were heated up breakfast.

' Boston Stump '—the lofty tower of the great pre-Reformation church of St. Botolph—stands up like a beacon across the Fen country.

It welcomed us several miles before we entered the narrow winding streets of this ancient town. I had been reading Cobbett's *Rural Rides* (one of the books which we had brought with us), and recalled what he had to say about " the fine open market place, nearly equal to that of Nottingham, good shops, good houses, pretty gardens about it, . . . the fine market for sheep, cattle, and pigs, and another for meat, butter and fish . . . a town of very considerable importance, and which is inhabited by people none of whom appear to be in misery."

Cobbett would find Boston had much changed if he could revisit it after a century. The trade is not what it was, and I fear that some of its inhabitants may be ' in misery ' or at least on the dole. Anyhow Cobbett would be glad to find the interior of the church is no longer " like a playhouse " and " disgraced by a gallery."

In startling contrast to St. Botolph's is the humble little ' Popish Chapel ' of Our Lady on the Horncastle Road of which I made a sketch.

33

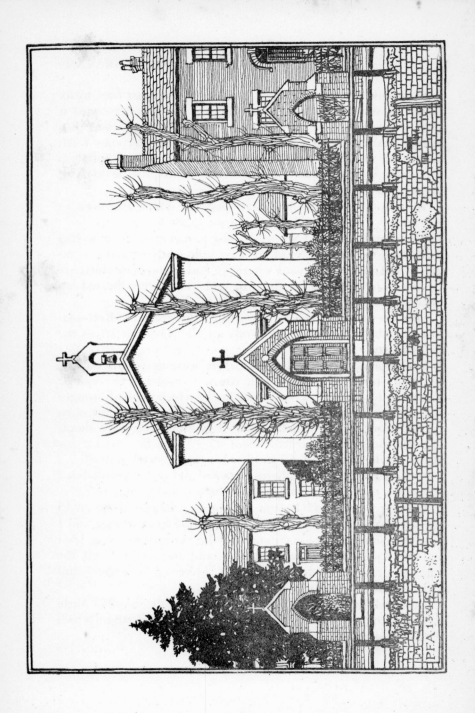

St. Mary's, Boston.

So complete was the triumph of Protestantism in this town, that in 1781 it was reported that "no Papists can be found here." At that time the few widely scattered Catholics were served by Jesuit missionaries. It was due to them that the severely plain 'chapel' was built. It overlooks one of the 'dykes' which help to give Boston more than a feeling of Holland.

We breakfasted in *Boston* and came to *New York* in time for lunch! American readers may not know these two places lie within a few miles of each other in Lincolnshire. The face of the country continued as before, low and level fenland, nearly all under cultivation. It was quite a relief when, early in the afternoon, we saw for the first time in four days, land rising above the level of the horizon.

I agreed with Cobbett—who rode through this same country, "that the sight had an effect like that produced by the first *sight of land* after a voyage across the Atlantic."

Then we got into an undulating country with low hills and wide valleys. About sunset we came to Horncastle, where just outside the town I found a farm where we were allowed to spend the night. The farmer said we had better stop in one of his fields, instead of going on further to a bit of common land where caravans generally stopped. "For you might find it rather awkward up there," said he. "Three gipsy vans came in yesterday, and I wouldn't say that you'd be welcomed, and might have a bit of trouble. They're a rough crowd."

I met some of the gipsies later on. They were returning from a pub, rather the worse for drink, and I came to the conclusion that they might have been a rowdy, and possibly too friendly neighbours if we had joined their camp.

Horncastle seemed to be a sleepy old town, but as we passed through its streets soon after 7 o'clock that February morning, perhaps it was rather early to form a fair impression of the place.

The snow still lay in patches on the fields, and got deeper as

35

the road climbed up on to the Wolds. It was only with difficulty that we managed to reach Panton College; the drive being blocked with snow in certain places. One of the boys had been sent out to look for the caravan. Under his direction Tony drove with caution, fearing that he might get stuck fast and be unable to move. It was a very desolate and wintry landscape we found on the Lincolnshire Wolds, exposed as they are to the full force of the wind.

But the warmth of the welcome given us by the Franciscan Fathers, some of whom were already waiting for us—a picturesque group in brown habits against a background on white snow—made up for the cold. In a few minutes the caravan had been dragged up a last steep bank to a bit of level ground near the stables, and the horses led away to a more distant field where it was to be hoped they would be able to find some patches of grass between the snow drifts.

Here I am taking the opportunity to put down all that we have seen and experienced since we were snowed up in the inn yard at Sutterton. Before I resume these notes I expect we shall be in Yorkshire. So I had better say something about this place where we are enjoying a week-end rest.

Panton Hall is a dignified 18th century mansion of red brick, set in the midst of a large park. The Capuchin Franciscans removed their school here from Cowley, near Oxford, in 1919. The vast stables were transformed into class rooms and dormitories for the elder boys. The younger ones were housed in the mansion itself. But if you visited Panton to-day you would not find either friars or school boys. Panton Hall has once more reverted to its original purpose as a country mansion, and the school has now been removed to Wyresdale Hall, near Lancaster. During the seventeen years the Capuchins were at Panton they did a great work in bringing back the Faith in rural Lincolnshire. Several new missions were started and the secular clergy could always rely on the friars to come to their aid when needed.

Panton Hall.

We spent three days at Panton and were entertained in that spontaneous and hospitable way which is characteristic of the sons of St. Francis all the world over. There was a delightfully ' homely ' atmosphere about the place. The boys, as might be expected, were curious to look inside the caravan, which was thrown open for inspection on the Sunday afternoon we were there. Certain boys who came from Ireland could not be kept away from the horses and wanted to ride them.

Church of the Holy Rood, Market Rasen.

FOUR

*Market Rasen—Osgodby—Brigg—Crowle—Goole—Howden
—Holme Hall—St. William's School, Market Weighton.*

The snow lay on the ground until the night before we left
Panton. Then a thaw started. When we set off again the
weather was mild and springlike; the roads deep in mud. Jack
and Bill were all the better for their three days rest. Jack, as
usual, gave us a lot of trouble before we got him harnessed, so
eager was he to start.

We came into unfrequented lanes, and after about three
hours, reached Market Rasen near midday   I stopped to make
a sketch of the more than a century old Catholic church, built
in 1824 by the last survivor of the post-Reformation English
Carmelite Missionaries, Fr. Francis Willoughby.

About two miles further on I told Tony to turn left from the
main road as I wanted to visit the secluded village of Osgodby.
Had I not been already told what to look out for I should
certainly have passed by the old red brick house which one
would never suspect to be a Catholic church.

This unspoilt example of a Penal Days ' Mass House ' was
built as long ago as 1793, by the Youngs of Kingerby Hall,
one of the few Lincolnshire families which held on to the old
Religion in spite of persecution, fines, and constant fear of
imprisonment.   Except for a cross on the roof—a modern addition—there is nothing to indicate that this plain two-storied
building is not an ordinary dwelling house, or possibly a school.
The chapel itself is to be found above the kitchen of the
presbytery.

If you want to realise what a typical Catholic chapel was like
in the Penal times—then visit Osgodby.   Here as nowhere else
do you manage to recapture the spiritual background of English
Catholic life two hundred years ago.

40

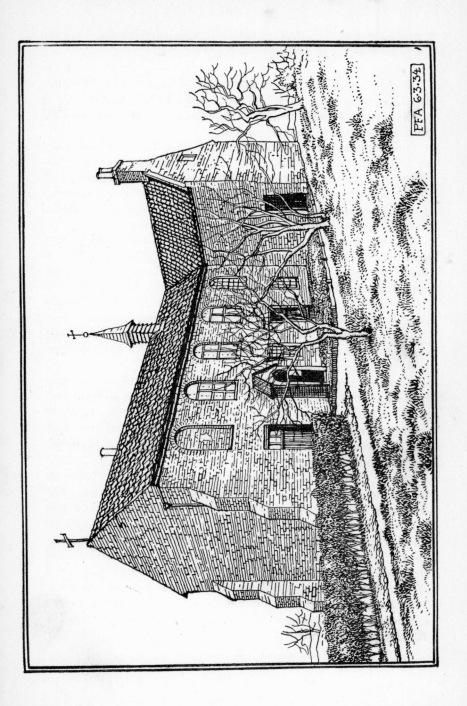

St. Mary and St. Joseph, Osgodby.

Brigg was our destination that night. In a direct line it could not have been more than ten miles away from Osgodby. But the lanes twisted and turned, so that the actual distance we had to cover must have about doubled.

Lincolnshire is still one of the most unchanged and unspoilt of English counties. As the caravan rumbled along that February afternoon through Thornton-le-Moor, South and North Kelsey, and other villages whose names I have forgotten, it would not have greatly surprised me if William Cobbett himself had appeared round a corner on his nag.

Of this very country he wrote in 1830 : " Large fields, fine pastures, flocks of those great sheep, of from 200 to 1,000 in a flock . . . never one single acre of waste land, and not one acre that would be called bad land in the south of England. . . . The *wolds,* or highlands, lie away to our right." But Cobbett complains that the ' almost total want of *singing birds* ' is a ' great drawback from the pleasure of viewing this fine country.' He notes that he heard nothing but a " little twittering from one thrush."

Towards evening the sky became overcast and within four miles of Brigg we got caught in a violent storm of rain and sleet. I had informed the superior of the Rosminian Convent of the arrival of the caravan. She had written to say that Jack and Bill would be welcome to graze in the playing fields adjoining the convent-school.

By the time we reached Brigg it was quite dark. I do not ever remember having such difficulty in finding our way. The field was approached by narrow streets which ended in a sort of yard, filled with objects whose exact nature could not be made out in darkness, relieved by neither moon, stars, or lamps. Here we decided to leave the caravan. When Jack and Bill were unharnessed we led them along a rough path, full of puddles and mud, until we reached the gate of the field. This was unfastened after some difficulty. Then having loosed the horses we refastened the gate and returned to the van for a late supper and bed.

St. Mary's, Brigg.

I found a very humble little Catholic church in Brigg. It had originally served as the stables of the Manor House, now turned into the Convent School. During the Penal Times the Faith was kept alive in this district by the Webb family at Worlaby Hall, where there was a chapel, generally served by the Franciscans. I learnt that the first public church was opened in Brigg about 1815, and that the present building was adapted as a place of worship by Mr. Valentine Cary-Elwes in 1874 after he had become a Catholic.

We set out the following morning about midday, having bought some pots of a delicious cherry jam which seems to be a speciality of this place.

Passing through the mushroom-growth red brick towns of Frodingham and Scunthorpe—which have recently sprung up around the iron and steel works—we descended a long hill and crossed over the sluggish Trent by a fine modern bridge.

A few years ago this northern part of Lincolnshire was given up entirely to agriculture. But now hundreds of acres of what were once corn fields have been scraped away for iron ore. For unlike the Cleveland district in Yorkshire, here the iron ore is found in the gravel soil of the surface, instead of being underground.

Once across the Trent we were on a long straight road with dead level fields on either side. The road itself was on a higher level than the surrounding land; a safeguard in times of flood. We found a camping ground without much trouble, but had to be careful in negotiating the sharp turn into the gate and the short drop into the grassy meadow.

Neither Tony nor I will forget that field in a hurry. We had planned an early start, and got up soon after dawn while a white mist still hung over the wide stretching Fens.

But Jack, always restive to be off, once he was in the shafts, upset all our carefully made preparations. That morning he seemed possessed by a devil. Before I had fastened the traces, and while Tony was still holding his head (a necessary pre-caution) he plunged forward more violently than usual. Various bits of harness snapped, and it was a wonder that he did not upset the van as he reared up.

Tony talked to him in language best left to the imagination. Then he roped him up to the wheel while he spent more than half an hour in repairing the damage with bits of string.

Once more we led Jack between the shafts, and before I had got the traces fastened, the same performance took place, with even more serious results. Tony got hold of some rope and gave Jack a little ' corporal chastisement ' which seemed to make him understand. With the aid of yet more bits of string the harness was lashed together.

Not wishing for any further adventures we decided to let Bill pull the van on to the road. He did so like a lamb. Then we unharnessed him and put back Jack into the shafts.

After nearly two hours delay we set off and three miles further on reached Crowle, where Tony was lucky to find a saddler who mended the damage and supplied new bits cf leather, where required.

While this was in progress I went off to make a drawing of St. Norbert's Church, which I found hidden away in a back street of this sleepy little town. The unusual dedication of this building is due to the fact that it belongs to the Premonstraten-sian Canons, who settled here in 1872. Before this the district was served from Gainsborough. The first Mass to be celebrated in Crowle since the Reformation took place nine years earlier. This is one of the poorest missions in the diocese of Notting-ham, and the Canons of St. Norbert must find it difficult to keep the Faith alive in this sleepy old town among the dykes and marshes.

When the harness had been mended we set off through dead level country that might have been Holland. It was a lovely spring morning, bright sunshine and a fresh breeze making the way seem shorter than if it had been raining. We ate our

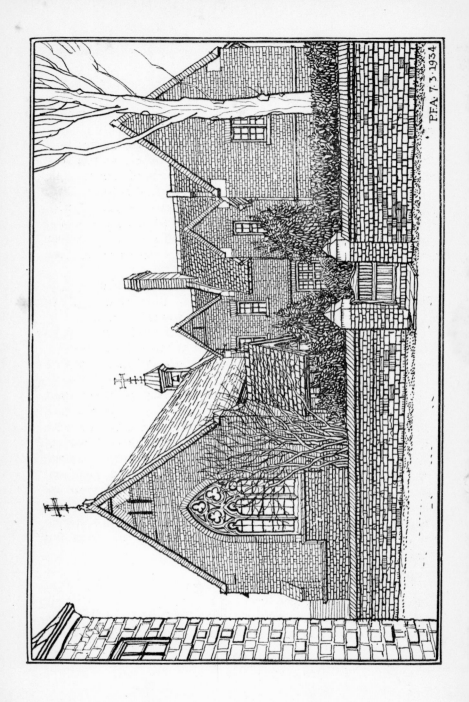

St. Norbert's, Crowle.

PFA. 7.3.1934

dinner by the side of a dyke, with the tall rushes murmuring in the breeze. Then rumbling on again, the caravan came into the village of Swinfleet on the Ouse. The river itself is hidden from the road by high banks erected as a safeguard in times of flood—once again recalling similar features in Holland.

The cobble-paved streets are what Tony and I chiefly remember about Goole; a drab and unattractive port, mainly devoted to the export of coal. The caravan bumped over these stones and I was thankful that I was not sitting on the driver's seat but walking on the pavement.

But I took the precaution to make sure that all the cupboard doors were fastened properly and that kettles and pans were removed from the stove on to the floor, otherwise the jolting of the waggon would have had disastrous results. On several previous occasions when I had forgotten to fasten the door of the ' china cupboard ' all its contents had fallen out! However the ' china ' was unbreakable—being enamelled tin ware. But I had to sweep up the sugar. Once it had got mixed up with the butter, and the contents of the coffee pot formed a dark brown pool on the mat. So I learnt to be careful of cobble stones.

We crossed the Ouse by the bridge at Booth Ferry and found ourselves in Yorkshire. It was now growing dusk. Having tried one or two farms and not managed to obtain grazing for the horses, we passed through Howden. Just beyond this peaceful old-world town, overshadowed by its Cathedral-like parish church, we secured a resting place for the night at a small dairy farm. Here we were given a real Yorkshire welcome. We ate our supper listening to the peal of bells, whose ringers were having a practice.

Very humble when compared to the pre-Reformation Catholic church of Howden is its modern successor. The first Catholic priest to settle in this town after an interval of nearly three centuries was the Rev. Robert Cook. When he arrived

Church of the Sacred Heart, Howden.

in Howden in 1852 so great was the fear of ' Popery ' that he was refused permission to say Mass in the Town Hall. Not to be put off he decided to preach in the streets, with such success, that it was not long before he was able to build a temporary chapel.

From Howden we took an unfrequented road across dead level country and about midday reached the village of Holme on Spalding Moor.

The word ' moor ' might suggest that it is situated on heather covered hills, but in this part of Yorkshire ' moor ' signifies waste-land. Such indeed was all this countryside until the bogs were reclaimed and turned into rich pasture land.

We turned in at the Lodge gates of Holme Hall, now a convent of the Third Order Franciscan Missionary Sisters of Mill Hill. The superior made us very welcome and while I was engaged drawing the chapel, the caravan rested in the front drive; the horses being let loose to graze in the park.

Until a few years ago Holme Hall belonged to the Stourtons, who were one of the great Yorkshire families who remained loyal to the Old Religion. The chapel, disguised externally as part of the stables, was built about 1670. The interior is a characteristic example of the classic style, and fortunately retains its original character, unspoilt by later additions. At the time of the French Revolution both the Canonesses of the Holy Sepulchre (now at New Hall, Essex) and the Passionist Fathers, found a temporary refuge in this rambling old mansion.

When the property was sold by the Stourtons in 1920 it became the novitiate for the Sisters whose apostolate lies in the Uganda missions. Part of the mansion is used as a guest house, and I can imagine no more delightful spot for a restful holiday than this historic Catholic stronghold, secluded from the world in the peaceful countryside of the Yorkshire plain.

From Holme Hall it was a short distance to St. William's School, our destination that night, whence we had received a most cordial invitation from the superior, Brother Finnbar to break our journey on the way north.

Holme Hall. The Chapel.

The large group of buildings were visible on our right, long before we reached them. As the caravan passed along the road several groups of boys, working in the fields, stopped to have a good look at this unusual object.

This well known Catholic Reformatory School for boys was founded in 1863. The Rosminian Fathers were placed in charge of it at first, taking over the property from the Franciscans, who found that its remote and isolated situation rendered it inconvenient as a centre for apostolic work. During more recent years the Reformatory (or as it now calls itself—an ' Approved School ') has been directed by the Brothers of the Christian Schools.

It is here that I am now writing, sitting at my little folding table inside the caravan, the stove burning brightly, and the lamp lit. It seems a long time since we left Panton; more like a month than a week. Tony has gone off to spend the evening with some of the boys, and I expect I shall be alone for an hour or two. So this is a good opportunity to bring my diary up to date.

During the week-end we have spent here there have been plenty of opportunities for us to learn something of the difficult responsibility which faces these self-sacrificing Irish Brothers in looking after the boys.

The type of lad who is sent to St. William's School invariably comes from the worst class of home. All of them have been convicted of some crime or other. It is no easy job to educate and reform these untrained minds and build up often half-starved bodies, or to instil them with even the most elementary notions of moral responsibility. It must be a disheartening task; one that demands not only an infinite experience of boys, but also an unlimited sense of humour.

On our arrival at the school one of the community told me never to leave the caravan door unlocked, for the Brothers could not be responsible if anything was ' pinched ' by the lads. But in spite of the fact that I sometimes forget the warning, and the boys have been in and out of the van the whole time, nothing has been taken so far.

Yesterday evening during our visit Mr. Water Wilkinson, whose delightful books are familiar to thousands of readers, gave one of his famous puppet shows to an enthusiastic audience. How the lads enjoyed themselves and how uproarious was the applause!

I am surprised to discover what a thoroughly good time these boys have, and it does not seem strange that many of them after they leave the school and have been found jobs elsewhere, run away and come back again. More often than not they just steal a car as being the easiest way to effect the return journey! Apparently they pine for the companionship of their own class. On the other hand some of the lads, particularly the elder ones, were all outspoken in their complaints about the discipline, and tell us that they hate being here. They long for the excitement of town life and get bored with the country.

On Saturday nights one of the Brothers accompanies the boys into Market Weighton where special seats are reserved for them at the local cinema. They are under no restrictions, and are allowed to walk home by themselves after the show is over. So long as they return at a certain time no questions are asked.

Each boy receives a small sum every week as pocket money, but fines are imposed for certain breaches of discipline. Smoking is allowed, and I gather that the weekly pocket money is generally spent on ' fags ' or sweets. Altogether everything is done to make the boys happy and content, and they are treated with the utmost kindness and consideration. Very different indeed is the modern Reformatory School to the grim prison-like institutions of half a century ago.

When talking to the various members of the community, all of whom are Irish, I cannot help feeling that they possess certain racial qualifications which enable them to carry out this sort of work far better than the average Englishman, and this afternoon I ventured to express my opinion.

" Yes : your're right," said one of the Brothers. " We did have an Englishman here for about six months. But he took

St. William's School, Market Weighton

PFA. 10. 3. 34.

everything far too seriously, and in the end had to be moved for his own good as well as for the sake of the boys. Perhaps our Irish sense of humour helps us in this sort of job—I'm not sure —anyhow we get on quite happily with the lads, and I'm sure I don't want to be shifted to teach in one of our ordinary schools, although I'm perfectly certain that the lessons I give here are probably mere waste of time from the purely human point of view."

He paused, and a look came into his eyes which made me realise that material success counted for very little to this Irish Brother; that to him, as to St. John Baptiste de la Salle, the founder of his Order, the will of God and his own personal sanctification came first, and that failure to produce ' results ' in education might even be more profitable when one has the gift of Faith to see God in all things, and to make one's daily life a continual sacrifice and penance.

The speaker was a man of brilliant intellect and wide read-ing—I found his knowledge of modern French literature and the classics far superior to my own—and yet here he was, to all intents and purposes, wasting his life teaching the rudimentary elements to boys of the lowest possible intelligence. And yet he was perfectly content to go on doing so as long as his superiors chose to keep him at this particular job.

I could write much more about St. William's School but we have still a long way to go and there are limits to this story of our caravan journey, so I must stop.

Within a short distance of Market Weighton there are many places of Catholic interest. Among them is Houghton Hall, the ancestral home of the Langdales, another old Yorkshire family which never lost the Faith.

Yesterday morning I made a sketch of its stately chapel, erected in 1829. It was rather sad to see this ornate structure in the Ionic style of classic architecture so badly in need of redecoration. It must have cost the Hon. Charles Langdale a small fortune to build, and at that time few Catholic chapels can have equalled it.

St. Mary's Everingham.

But an even more magnificent chapel is to be found at Everingham, the seat of the Constable family, who, like their neighbours, the Stourtons and Langdales, always refused to conform to Protestantism. The present chapel was opened in 1839, and erected at the cost of William Constable-Maxwell, who afterwards became Lord Herries. He was the ancestor of the dowager Duchess of Norfolk, to whom Everingham now belongs, as she is Baroness Herries in her own right.

It is almost impossible to convey in a small drawing the rich and costly decorations of the interior of this chapel, with its fluted Corinthian columns of marble, elaborate brass work, and sculpture. This mission is now served by the Canons Regular of the Lateran.

I have also visited Beverley during this week-end at St. William's School, in order to sketch the modern Catholic church. The mission dates from 1846. Four years later Beverley became the territorial see of the Bishop of the old Yorkshire district on the restoration of the Hierarchy. But the Bishops continued to live at York, and no attempt was made to erect even a ' pro-cathedral ' in this old market town, whose glorious pre-Reformation minster it would have been impossible to emulate. The diocese of Beverley ceased to exist in 1878 when it was divided between the two sees of Leeds and Middlesbrough

FIVE

*York—Easingwold—Kilvington—Osmotherley—Guisborough
—The Moorland Road—Ugthorpe.*

Our next stopping place was York, and the twenty miles journey there from St. William's School, Market Weighton was far from being a joyride. The weather was cold and stormy. There were frequent showers of rain. The country was dull and featureless. We passed through Everingham and Sutton on Derwent. By 4 o'clock we got to Osbaldwick, to-day an outlying suburb of York. Here we were lucky in being able to spend the night in the yard behind the Derwent Arms, where we found a friendly innkeeper.

The next morning we were away in good time. Tony found it a tricky job piloting his caravan and two horses through the narrow streets of York. Having reached a convenient parking place just in front of the Minster we stopped for breakfast; the police raising no objection to our presence.

On the opposite of the street, a few yards away, was St. Wilfrid's Catholic Church, which I had not time to sketch as we were anxious to be at Easingwold by midday. For this same reason I had to ignore the three other Catholic churches in the city, and the much more interesting Bar Convent, the first community of nuns to be established in England after the Reformation. It was founded by Mrs. Bedingfield in 1680. Its chapel contains many relics of the York Martyrs who laid down their lives for The Faith during the Penal Times.

When we had finished breakfast and Jack and Bill had eaten their bags of corn and had a drink of water, we moved on again, taking the main road, northwards. Nothing unusual occurred during the forenoon, and not being a farmer I found

St. John's, Easingwold.

the endless ploughed fields somewhat uninteresting.

At Easingwold we were welcomed in the true Benedictine spirit by Dom Hilary Willson, titular Cathedral Prior of Rochester, who has been in charge of this mission for several years. Fr. Hilary had already made all arrangements for the caravan to be parked in a yard adjoining a baker's shop. Everything was prepared for our visit, including fresh straw and hay in the stable. No detail had been forgotten for the comfort of man and beast.

I made a sketch of St. John's Church, designed by Joseph Hansom in 1830, a typical example of the early Gothic Revival.

Fr. Hilary told me its history; how previous to 1830 the Catholics of Easingwold used to worship in the house-chapel at Crayke, some two miles away. Before this they heard Mass at Oulston, where the widow of the 4th Viscount Fauconburg of Newburgh Priory, generally managed to keep a priest.

St. John's is a homely little church. The rood screen was removed here from St. Anne's, Liverpool; another mission, which like Easingwold, has always been served by the Benedictine monks of Ampleforth Abbey.

The following morning, after Mass and breakfast, Fr. Hilary said he would like to accompany us on our journey, as he was afraid we might not be able to discover Chapel House Farm, North Kilvington, where the Meynell family kept alive the old Religion in this part of Yorkshire.

This was the first and only occasion when the caravan had a priest as passenger. Fr. Hilary soon made himself at home, sitting by the stove, (for the morning was cold and raw) where he said his office with as much recollection and unconcern as if he had been in his stall in choir. When he had finished this obligation he got out and walked for two or three miles while I did my best to prepare a lunch which would be worthy to set before such a distinguished guest. The menu was tomato soup, cold ham and salad, cheese, fruit and coffee. The choice was limited, for cooking when a caravan is rumbling and swaying is not an easy job, as the contents of pots and pans are liable to spill over the stove at any sudden bump on the road or change in the pace of the horses.

We stopped near Thirkelby for lunch, to which the Cathedral Prior of Rochester did full justice. Passing through the town of Thirsk where I paid a brief visit to the Catholic church in charge of the Capuchin Fathers. We arrived at a gate leading into a field, at the far end of which was a grey stone farmhouse. Fr. Hilary introduced us to the farmer who said we would be welcome to spend the night here, and showed us a field where the horses could graze.

It is uncertain when the farmhouse and chapel were built, probably early in the 18th century. From the main-road there is nothing to show that the greater part of the building consists of a chapel, so cleverly is it concealed. Only when one gets round to the back does one notice some rather unusually large windows. The adjoining sacristy might be taken for an outhouse.

Benedictines, Jesuits, and secular priests served this ancient mission at one time or another. But the scattered congregation gradually decreased until it decided that it would be more convenient to erect a church in Thirsk. For some years past St. Anne's, Kilvington has been closed and Mass is no longer said here.

Fr. Hilary said goodbye to us, returning to Easingwold by bus. We spent a peaceful night in a field near the farm. The following morning, having purchased milk, butter and eggs, we set off northwards.

The Cleveland Hills lay on the right; the country becoming wilder and more rugged. After about six miles I told Tony to stop, for there was a sign post pointing the way to Osmotherley. Bidding him wait here for an hour or so I set off on foot, up a hilly road.

Passing a woman coming in the opposite direction I asked

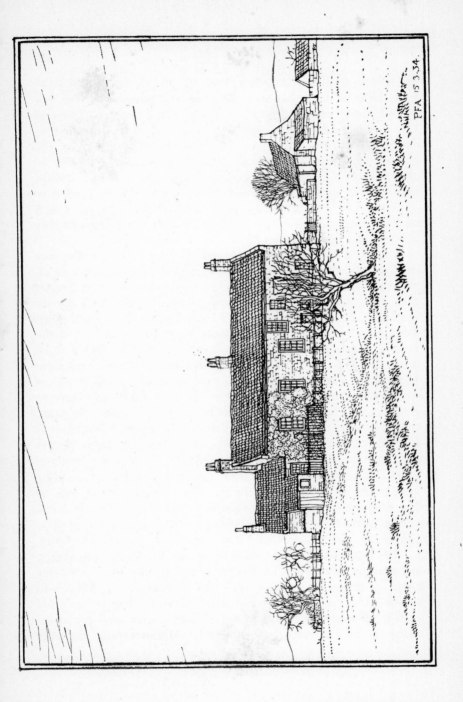

St. Anne's, Kilvington.

her how to find the Catholic chapel.

A smile lit up her face on learning my request. "Aye, it's a good thing you met me," she said "for I keep the key and I've got it here in my bag." I explained that I wanted to make a drawing and that it would be appearing in the *Universe*. This announcement greatly excited her. "Oh: I always look at yon drawings every week. We'll be very proud here to see our little church in the paper." She proceeded to give me minute directions how to find the chapel, which semed rather superfluous, considering the fact that Osmotherley is no more than a tiny village.

But when I got there I realised she had good reason, for the Catholic church—if it can be so called—consists of a small room on the top floor of a large three storied stone house, now used as a Bank. It is approached at the back by an outside stair. Few places I have visited in England have given me such a vivid idea of what it meant to be a Catholic in the Penal times than this Upper Room at Osmotherley, which might be described as the "*Coenaculum*" of the Yorkshire Moors. I sincerely hope that the diocesan authorities of Middlesborough will never allow this venerable sanctuary to pass out of Catholic hands or to be used for secular purposes.

It was about 1672 that the Franciscans opened a school at Osmotherley ,which for nearly 150 years remained their mother house in England. In this secluded village on the Cleveland Hills the novices underwent that severe training and discipline which was to fit them for their future life as missionaries, or for martyrdom. St. Francis himself would have felt at home in this little friary where conditions must often have been as poverty stricken as at Our Lady of the Angels or Rivo Torto.

The Franciscans left Osmotherley in 1823 and since then the number of resident Catholics has slowly dwindled. To-day there is no resident priest, and only occasionally is Mass said in the " Upper Room " by a priest from Stokesley.

Within a mile or two from the village are the well preserved ruins of the Carthusian monastery of Mount Grace; the only

"The Upper Room," Osmotherley.

pre-Reformation Charterhouse in England of which any extensive remains now exist.

But time did not allow me to make a pilgrimage to Mount Grace. I had already kept my companion waiting nearly two hours at the cross roads and when I got back I was glad to find dinner was ready for me. It was not often that Tony had a chance to show off his gifts as a *chef*. His speciality was fried bacon, but I have known him to produce some original kinds of soup and stews. I never discovered if he could make Yorkshire pudding.

During the afternoon the horses plodded along, dragging their heavy load through Ingleby, Stokesley, and Great Ayton. The weather was unsettled. More than one drenching shower made driving extremely unpleasant. Yorkshire had given us a very moist welcome since we entered its broad acres.

After leaving Ayton I called at several farms in search of camping ground, but with no success. I wanted Tony to try his luck with his fellow countrymen—for he was now in his native Cleveland Hills. But he doubted if he would fare any better even if he could speak the same language as the farmers.

By the time we crossed the railway bridge at Pinchingthorpe it was quite dark and we had to light the lamps. If there was one thing Tony disliked, and with good reason, it was driving at night. Neither did Jack and Bill care for the blinding glare of motor car headlights.

At last, very weary and not in the best of tempers, we reached Guisborough, where, thanks to my companion's intimate know ledge of the less fashionable quarters of the capital of Cleveland, he managed to find a back yard of a low-class inn, not likely to be " starred " by the A.A., where we were allowed to stop the night. The small space available was already half occupied by another caravan, whose owners were real gipsies, not amateur vagrants like our two selves. However they proved to be quite friendly, although I expect they were some what puzzled to know what to make of us.

The road from Guisborough to Ugthorpe had been the subject of long discussion between Tony and myself. It climbs up several hundred feet on to the moors, and its gradients are not such as one would attack with a heavily laden horse-drawn caravan. It was very doubtful if Jack and Bill would be able to manage these 'banks.' The worst and longest of them could be avoided by taking a circuitous route through Boosbeck and Lingdale. So we decided to do this.

Bill was put on in tandem at each of the steep 'banks' and I admit there were one or two bad moments when we thought the horses would stop before reaching the top.

But all went well and as it was a glorious morning with a bright sun, blue sky, and fresh breeze, we felt very cheerful when we found ourselves on the moors with the sea far away on our left and endless stretches of heather on our right.

We were making good time and had no doubt that we should reach Ugthorpe before sunset. But suddenly, without any warning, one of the shafts broke in two with a painfully audible sound of splitting timber as Tony was driving down a slight hill. He shoved on the brake and managed to stop the heavy load from pressing forward on to the horses.

We were miles from any village, with no sign of human habitation, except a small farm about quarter of a mile to the right of the road. Tony asked me to go and see if the owner would allow the horses to be put into one of his fields, for we could not let them loose on the heather or bog. The farmer consented on hearing of our mishap. I returned to the van. Tony led Jack to the field, while I followed with Bill.

Tony decided that he had better go off to find a blacksmith. I remained in sole charge of the van and to keep an eye on the horses who were in range of view.

The afternoon dragged on rather slowly. I killed time by cleaning and polishing every bit of brass work within and without the caravan. I had my tea and then lit the lamps. It was now quite dark, and still no sign of Tony who had been absent for over four hours. The wind began to rise, and before half an hour had passed, it had increased to the force of a gale. The caravan swayed and rocked like a small vessel at anchor in a heavy sea. I began to wonder if my ' ship on wheels ' would hold fast or would be blown over. From time to time a fierce squall of driving rain and sleet added to the excitement.

Eight o'clock came and still no sign of Tony. Had he got lost on the moors, or had he decided to spend the night with his parents in the village of Brotton, about five miles distant from where he had been stranded? There was nothing to be gained by waiting up for my companion, so I came to the conclusion that bed would be the most comfortable place on such a night.

I lay there in the darkness while the van creaked and swayed as each gust of wind attacked it. I cannot recall any more eerie experience in my whole life than that wild night spent alone in a gipsy caravan stranded on a moorland road.

It was not until about midday that Tony returned, smiling and cheerful as usual. He had been unable to find a blacksmith the previous afternoon, so when the storm got up, felt he had better spend the night at Brotton. He had brought a man with him who managed to mend the broken shaft. This done, we proceeded on our journey amid more heavy showers of rain and sleet.

Somehow or other Jack and Bill surmounted the worst ' bank ' on the road just beyond the ' Jolly Sailor ' Inn. But it was an alarming business and we breathed a sigh of relief when, sweating and panting they reached the summit.

On again, the road rising and falling like a switch back. The weather could not have been more unpleasant, for rain and sleet had turned to wet snow which made the road tarmac surface very dangerous for the horses, especially as its surface was almost as smooth as glass, with nothing to give them a grip.

At last we came to a sign post marked UGTHORPE. We knew

this was the last lap on our long journey of more than three hundred miles since leaving the Thames Valley. Tony urged on the horses for a final effort. We passed an old windmill, descended a short hill, and drew up at the ' Black Bull ' Inn.

Like most of the older houses in the lonely moorland village, it is built of greenish grey stone. The low pitched roof is covered with red tilings. The walls are thick, and the winter storms cannot penetrate them. Behind the inn are the stables opening on to a yard where on summer evenings you will find the village men playing quoits. But March is not the month for outdoor amusements on the Yorkshire moors. So there was room in the yard for the caravan, and here it remained, while Jack and Bill roamed where they liked in a large field of several acres, with nothing to do but grow fat and lazy.

Ugthorpe, which was to be our headquarters for the next five weeks, is a scattered hamlet on the moors, about eight miles from Whitby. Thanks to the staunch Catholicism of the Radcliffes and the moorland farmers, this district has always remained a stronghold of the Faith; a little Catholic oasis in the midst of a desert of Protestantism.

The surrounding countryside is closely bound up with the life of the Venerable Nicholas Postgate, who was martyred at York in 1679. In the church at Ugthorpe are preserved two chalices used by the martyr. At Egton, where Fr. Postgate used to say Mass, until recent years stood the Old Chapel, now pulled down and rebuilt as a modern cottage.

The first permanent chapel to be built at Ugthorpe was erected in 1708. It was replaced by another—now used as the parish hall—in 1810. The present Gothic church—often called the ' Cathedral of the Moors '—was erected by the well-known Mr. Thomas Rigby, who was in charge of the mission from 1835 to 1889. It was opened by Cardinal Wiseman in 1857. The large group of buildings next the church was used as a boys' school for many years; most of the sons of the Catholic farmers in the north of Yorkshire being educated here at one time.

St. Anne's, Ugthorpe.

P.F.A. 7.4. 1934.

For many years Ugthorpe was served by the Missionaries of the Sacred Heart, but in 1936 it was once again put in charge of the secular clergy.

There are not many villages in England, outside Lancashire, where one finds a real ' native ' type of Catholicism flourishing as it does at Ugthorpe. It would be a revelation to many Anglicans, who regard ' Romanism ' as a kind of religion unsuited to the ' Nordic temperament,' to live at Ugthorpe for a few weeks. Here they would find sturdy Yorkshire folk whose ancestors have been Catholics from time immemorial, and who cannot imagine belonging to any other kind of religion than that in which they have been born and bred. They are as proud of being Catholics as of being Yorkshiremen, and make no pretence of looking down with a certain contempt—if one may use the word—upon everyone else who does not share in these privileges!

The outward expression of their Faith is as natural and spontaneous as that of a Breton peasant or Italian ' *contadino*.' In many a farmhouse you will still find the family saying the Rosary together before going to bed at night. On a Sunday morning you will meet the young farm lads and lassies cycling to church from miles around on their way to Mass and Holy Communion. On a Saturday night you will find the men at Confession—and it does not seem anything unusual to meet them later on, in the crowded bar of the village inn, enjoying a pint of beer or exchanging the latest gossip. There are whist drives and dances too, for Ugthorpe knows how to amuse itself during the long winter evenings.

In this Yorkshire village, still very much cut off from the world in spite of motor buses which in recent years have made it less isolated, one can form a picture in one's mind of what every village in England would be like if the Reformation had not taken place. The Catholicism of Ugthorpe is as much part of the place as the stone farmhouses, the stone dykes and the rolling moors.

SIX

*Finding a new caravan—a deal with gipsies—exchange of
wagons—preparations.*

After our arrival at Ugthorpe I started to work out the route
we should follow on the long journey to and from the north of
Scotland.   I spent hours poring over maps and Contour Road
Books.

Our van, when fully loaded, weighed over two tons—far too
much for anything but level country.   Every gipsy we had met
on the roads had always warned us that this wagon was too
heavy, even for two horses, and advised us to get a lighter one.
The alternative seemed to be a light rulley, surmounted by a few
' spars ' of bent wood; the whole top covered with canvas.   The
interior arrangements would be much the same, but there would
be less space, height, and ventilation; the latter restricted to a
tiny window at the back and a window above the door at the
front.

After much argument, Tony and I finally decided that we
must get rid of the luxurious and comfortable ' Portiuncula '
which had been our home for the past eight months.   A lighter
wagon would solve the road problem.   With it we could ignore
all but the steepest gradients.   We should be able to cover a
distance of twenty to thirty miles a day without having to pick
out level roads.

Tony now set to work to make friends with all the gangs of
gipsies or half-breed gipsies, within a radius of fifty miles.   At
a neighbouring market-town, he chanced to meet one of these
typical half-breed gipsies, whom I will call ' Kale Marshall.'
He and his gang were, so it appeared, always willing to sell or
trade anything—horses, cattle, carts, vans, rags, bottles, bones—
in fact the landlord of the ' Black Bull ' told us that if either

of us wanted a wife, Kale would be able to provide a selection of possible candidates for a consideration!

So one morning Tony went off to meet the famous Kale Marshall in person. That same afternoon he returned home accompanied by two gipsies. Kale himself is best described as a small dirty rat of a man with a rough bristle of black sprouting hair over his mouth and jaws. His trousers were ragged. A grey woollen shirt, much patched, and open at the neck, a faded ' sports jacket ' (which might have been picked off a dust heap), and an old black felt hat, completed his costume.

He told me he had come to see our van, so I took him round to the back of the inn to have a look at it, reminding him that it was West Hartlepool built (this is where the best vans come from) and that it was in as good a condition as when we bought it less than a year ago. He remarked that he had already seen the van when we had passed through Guisborough a few weeks back, saying that he liked the look of our pair of " good little hosses," enquiring if we would like to sell one of them.

" Certainly not! " was my reply.

Kale and his companion examined the van with critical glances—first the exterior, then the interior.

" Well! " he drawled, " she's a good 'un. What d'you want for her? If you'd like to swop, I dare say I can find another without you having to pay a bit extra. There's not many folk round here who'd need a wagon like this for travelling. She's too heavy. But she's all right for living in. I'll see what I can do for you."

" Tell you what," I interrupted, " if you'll take on the job for us, I'll pay you a commission. How will that suit you? "

" That'll be all right for me, sir. You can trust me to put through the deal on my own! "

" But understand," I replied, " I must see the other van myself before we agree to swop."

Kale said this was quite fair. He told me he would run over again when he had had a good look round, saying that he thought he could find just the right sort of van in one or two

71

places he knew of.

" There's two young friends of mine that's just got married," he went on to explain." There's likely to be one more in the family before very long, so they'll be glad of a bit more room.'

So shaking hands with the two men, I watched them drive off in one of the most ramshackle and dilapidated old Ford cars that I have ever set eyes on.

The days passed quickly. Tony spent most of the time working at his horses, while I had other jobs to keep me busy. It was a pleasure to go out into the fields and watch him. Jack and Bill were real gipsy-looking nags by now. They had not lost their winter coats. I doubt if they had slept in a stable more than two nights since we had bought them. They could live on rough food. They could be loosed out on any road, no matter how busy it was with traffic. No motor-car seemed to frighten them. At night they could be put in among other horses, and be trusted to look after themselves. They never strayed far in the day time, and always came back on their own.

Jack was the more shy of the two. After the couple of months running wild in the open, he needed breaking in again, so Tony had a strenuous job. At one time someone must have treated Jack badly, for when we first got him he could not stand being touched on the head. But he soon got over this.

Bill, unlike Jack, trusted everybody. He would come to any-one who called him. He would stand like a rock when Tony fluttered bits of paper in his face. He seemed to realise that it was merely a silly game, and that there would be a lump of sugar as a reward! But Tony liked Jack the better of the two horses. He was the stronger, and had more spirit and fighting temper. He never gave in, and once he had learned to trust his driver and master, he would follow him everywhere, doing anything he was ordered.

Bill was different. He was slow and rather stupid. A sharp word would often frighten him, in spite of his normal confidence in men, maybe just because one seldom had to speak sharply to him. It seemed to break his heart to be corrected. He just couldn't make it out. But these two horses, so utterly unlike in temperament, made an ideal pair. If Tony ever changed their places they used to start fighting. Each seemed to know his own job, and resented the other usurping it.

During the months of idleness at Ugthorpe they were getting fat and putting on flesh. But Tony remarked to me that this fat would soon leave them after a week or two on the roads. " A skinny horse," he would say, " is no good to sell, but a fat horse is no good for work. Looks are nothing on the roads; it's results that count.

Tony would disappear after breakfast, and never return until dinner time. The days were all too short for what he had to do with his nags before they would be ready for their long journey to Scotland. Sometimes the local farmers would come and talk to him while he was working at the horses; proffering good advice and asking questions.

One Sunday morning there was an unusual sound outside the inn. We looked out of the window and discovered that it was our friend, Kale Marshall, together with two other gipsies, in their ramshackle old ' bus.' We went down to receive them.

" How have you got on? " I enquired.

" I want you to come along with us at once," was his answer. " I've several vans for you to look at. Now, I'd better tell you that you may have to pay a bit extra. It's like this—we use these little vans for going through the country. That van of yours is out-of-date; in fact you'll never see one up north that isn't pulled by an engine. Mind you, I don't say she won't do for the job if anybody would yoke plenty of power to her. But even two strong nags like yours take a lot of keeping, and even they aren't strong enough. 'Course, the van could be converted to use with an engine, but that'd cost too much. Rubber tyres, and another sort of steering. I've seen a lot of fellows. They're all willing to swop, but you'll have to pay them a bit extra."

I looked at Tony. It was clear that he was surprised and annoyed.

" What about it? Shall we be going? " I asked him.

" May as well. We're not forced to buy or even swop " was his brief comment.

So we all got into the old Ford, and were soon rattling along the road to the market town, some thirty miles away, where about two hours later we drove into an open yard which was full of gipsy vans of all shapes, sizes and colour. Broken untidy wagons, beautiful and brightly painted wagons—in fact every type of caravan which could be imagined. Some were of crazy workmanship and primitive brush work, with large wheels as big as those of a steam roller or old fashioned dog-cart; others with two small wheels at the front and two large ones at the back. The vans were ranged round the sides of the yard, close together. In the centre was an open space. Many of them had recently been repaired and repainted in readiness for the summer, which meant taking the road again after having been laid up during the winter.

Dogs of all inter-mixed breeds and colour lolled under the bodies of the vans. Dark-eyed and swarthy skinned children played on the steps, or on the ground. It was near dinner-time and a smell of cooking hung over the yard. Through the open doors of some of the wagons could be seen women bending over the stoves. As we passed by they looked up and glared at us with keen-eyed curiosity. From each small chimney a thin column of blue smoke arose, only to be borne away aloft. Mingled with the smell of cooking was the unmistakable odour of unwashed humanity and frowsty clothes.

At one end of the yard was a group of men and lanky youths; all dressed in shabby old suits. Black soft felt hats were worn by most of them. Around each neck was the inevitable scarf of vivid colour. They were talking among themselves. I could only make out a low indistinct murmur.

Kale Marshall stopped at one of the wagons.

" Here's one I think may suit you " he said. " Have a look

at her."

I did so. The van was a shabby old thing, and I was not much impressed.

Kale kicked the wheels; banging the timbers, saying as he did so, "Sound as a bell! Now sir, your two 'hosses' would pull this little 'un like winkin'".

"What's the inside like?" I asked, pulling aside the coarse canvas curtain which closed the entrance instead of the usual door. The interior proved to be completely empty, except for a very dilapidated stove and two cupboards, one with a broken door.

"She's no good!", Tony interrupted. "Look! No brakes —two broken felloes—three thin tyres—rotten bottom! It looks as if she'd been on the road for about a century. Come on, Kale! When you're ready, we'll see a decent van or two. Junk's no good for us!"

So we were led to another van, which was occupied by an elderly couple who were about to sit down to their Sunday dinner. They invited us to step inside and have a look round. This van was very poorly furnished, with nothing but the barest necessities, and no attempt at comfort. A single bunk, convertable into a double bed at night; a rickety, much patched-up stove, which wafted as much smoke out of its broken chimney as passed through into the open air. A curtain hung across from one side to the other made two 'rooms,' but there was really hardly large enough space for one person. Looking at the tiny cupboards I doubted if they would hold more than my pencils and paints, certainly not my portfolios of drawing paper!

"How d'you like this wagon?" Kale asked. "Better than the last, isn't she?"

"Not large enough for our needs," was all I could answer.

"Any more rubbish to show us?" enquired Tony.

"Come and see this 'un at the top." was Kale's reply. He led us across the yard to a van we had not yet seen. I climbed the steps, and entered the door. Here I found a young couple in possession. Everything was spotless. Brasses shining, the furniture and linoleum fragrant with polish; the stove newly black-leaded. Altogether a perfect little home. I gazed round and noticed drawers, cupboards, and shelves. Dainty curtains of orange silk framed the bed, while others of flowered muslin decked the windows. There were vases of artificial flowers on the mantle-shelf above the stove. So far as I was concerned, this van quite satisfied my own requirements. But it was Tony's business to find out if the wheels and base were in good condition.

He then proceeded to examine the outside carefully, the " gang " standing by, and saying nothing. He shook his head, remarking that he didn't quite like the look of one of the springs—it seemed a bit worn. So this wagon was rejected like all the others we had seen so far.

Kale then led us to yet another van. Tony and I explored the inside while the men stopped without. I confess I was even more satisfied with this one than the former. There were two bunks; double and single. Two long drawers at the side of the bottom bunk which I realised would hold all my drawing materials, and much else besides. The usual folding table, complete with a drawer and a cupboard beneath, where groceries could be stowed away. A good stove and a small oven, above which ran a polished mahogany mantle-piece, adorned with no less than eight mirrors. At the top was fastened a long string of glass beads, which swayed and tinkled against the mirrors whenever one made the slightest movement. A corner cupboard, just right for china (actually tin mugs and plates). At the opposite side a wardrobe. The floor was covered with linoleum. The only features I did not like were the low roof, and the lack of proper ventilation, when compared with the many windows and skylights in the " Portiuncula." Here the roof was made of canvas, stretched over wooden ribs, painted green on the outside. The inside of the canvas was covered with red rep which gave the interior a most cheerful appearance. Most of the cupboards and lockers were made of three-ply wood, which all helped to reduce weight. In our own van all the woodwork was mahogany.

I have described this van in detail for it was to be our home for the next four months. I told Tony it would do all right so far as I was concerned, and as he seemed to be satisfied with the undercarriage and wheels we decided to take it.

However the business of exchanging our heavy wagon for this light one was a long drawn out affair, for you may be sure the gipsies wanted to drive a hard bargain.

Now that they knew we had found a van to suit us, they protested that they would be incurring a dead loss if they parted with the little van in exchange for the " Portiuncula." They pointed out with most convincing logic that *two* horses would be quite superfluous; that one horse would pull a light canvas cover van up any hill—so they would be satisfied if we would hand over the big caravan AND one of our horses.

It would take too long to relate the whole story of that afternoon spent in haggling over money. We eventually adjourned to a neighbouring public house and settled the business over a pint of beer each. I must confess that after three or four hours the gipsies had beaten me in a game which they could play far better than either myself or Tony, and I agreed to pay them £10 in addition to exchanging vans. Of course it was sheer robbery on their part, but they knew I wanted this particular van, and quite rightly, they themselves were determined to get the best of the bargain.

Before returning to Ugthorpe we agreed to meet at a certain spot where they would bring the van and hand it over in exchange for ours. I spent two days in cleaning out the contents of all the drawers and cupboards, retaining the cushions and curtains.

After an early breakfast Tony drove off, and I watched the " Portiuncula " disappear from sight along the moorland road. I had grown very much attached to this home on wheels in which we had lived for nearly eight months. It was so comfortable and convenient in every way. I bitterly regretted having to part with it, for I realised only too well, that no matter what we might gain by having a lighter and less cumbersome wagon, the latter would never quite compensate for the lack of space and domestic conveniences.

Late in the evening Tony arrived home with the new van. He told me that it seemed as light as a feather to the horses, especially Jack, who bounded along with quick steps and more lengthy strides. He said that he had to keep on touching Bill's flanks with the reins to prevent him from jabbing himself on the corner of the van. The difference in weight was simply marvellous. He said that the gipsies had tried their utmost to persuade him to part with one of our nags, again pointing out that we should not need him any longer. Altogether the drive home had been an exciting experience. The horses went at an alarming speed; climbing the steep hills easily, and once over the top, " a running and busting themselves to get on." They took the dips in the road at a gallop, and the momentum thus gained, carried the van up the other side almost as easily as it went down.

Next morning Tony took me to have a look at our new home by daylight. Examining the wheels with the eye of a professional, he came to the conclusion that the gipsies must have put on old ones before they had parted with the van, because he would have sworn that these were not the same rims or tyres which we had seen when we first saw it. He was so indignant at having been fooled that he decided to interview Kale Marshall and his gang without any further delay, and give them a piece of his mind.

" Don't you worry " he exclaimed. " I'll slip along to-day. I'll get 'em. It's a dirty trick they've played us."

Not only the wheels, but also the stove within the van appeared to have been tampered with. For on examining the latter I found that the iron plates at the back were broken. But it was not so easy to prove that this damage had not been there when we had looked over the van in the first instance.

Tony failed to get any satisfaction from his interview with Kale Marshall, who swore that the wheels were in exactly the same condition as when we first saw the van, and that he knew nothing about the stove. Of course we had no definite proof and he knew it all right.

We spent nearly a week working on the van before we set off for Scotland. Tony oiled the wheels, and re-painted the outside, while I spent many hours scrubbing and polishing the interior. Then we had to pack up everything we needed for our long journey; clothes, books, maps, kitchen utensils, tin plates and mugs, knives and forks, spoons, bedding and blankets, not forgetting my typewriter and the new portable wireless.

How to stow them all away in about half the space of the former wagon was a problem. There were moments when I felt I should never be able to endure living in such uncomfortable and cramped quarters. Groceries were purchased and then at last came the morning for our departure. Jack and Bill were brought in from their field and harnessed. We were expecting the former might give trouble but he was fairly quiet when put into the shafts.

Our friends in the village came to see us off, and as Tony drove away gave us a ringing cheer. " We'll be back again in three months time if all goes well " I said to them. And thanks to Tony's care of his nags and no serious disasters we kept to our scheduled time table, returning to the " Black Bull " on the very date I had anticipated.

PART II

SEVEN

*Stockton—Croxdale—Ushaw College—Durham—Newcastle—
Morpeth—Longhorsley.*

I am writing up my diary at Ushaw College.   The caravan
is in a corner of the farmyard behind a barn.   We arrived
here yesterday afternoon having set off from Ugthorpe three
days ago.   There is half a gale blowing and to prevent the
wagon from swaying as each gust of wind meets it we have
propped it up with poles.   The little stove is giving out a
terrific heat, and the interior of the van is almost unendurably
stuffy, for as I have already stated, there is no means of ventilation except one leaves open the top half of the door or the
tiny window above the bed.   If both these are open there is
a fierce draught.

On leaving Ugthorpe we realised that our new wagon had
a quite different motion to its predecessor.   It was the
difference between a destroyer and a battleship, or a motor
side-car and a steam roller.   In the ' Portiuncula' you were
always conscious of its *weight;* in the new van you could never
forget its *lightness.*   The horses were aware of the difference
in the load they were pulling.   For the first five miles we
rattled along at an alarming rate.   Note the verb ' rattled '—
for up to this moment I have always used ' rumbled ' to express
the motion of the ' Portiuncula.'   Up and down hills we went
without stopping.   The moor road might have been almost
dead level instead of series of switch backs.
Within the van, where I was engaged making things ' ship-
shape ' I felt I was being shaken to pieces and wondered if I

80

St. Mary's, Stockton.

should ever get used to this nerve and body-racking motion. Everything rattled and creaked; the floor, the door, the cupboards, the tin plates and mugs; and above all the glass bead fringe which adorned the glass mirror above the stove. Realising that their jangling could be stopped, even if nothing could be done to lessen the other noises, I pulled them down.

Mile after mile we covered at a pace which seemed incredible when compared to what we had been accustomed for the past six months. Down the steep ' Blue Bank ' and on through Guisborough by slower stages, for by this time the horses were beginning to show signs of weariness, until we reached a farm at Nunthorpe, where we spent the night. It was here that we first made use of the portable wireless set which had now been added to the furniture of the van. And it was quite pleasant that fine May evening to listen to a concert after supper.

Hoping to reach Durham before sunset, we made an early start the following morning, stopping by the blacksmith's shop in Marton for our breakfast. Here Tony bought a stock of nails for the horses' shoes, always having to be renewed as they soon wore down on the smooth road surface.

Then moving on again we passed through Thornaby and Stockton, where the cobbled streets gave the driver some painful moments.

While the horses were having a rest I made a quick sketch of St. Mary's, Norton Road, the oldest of Stockton's three Catholic churches. The mission dates from about 1790, and the present church was erected in 1842 from the designs of Augustus Welby Pugin. But I fear he would scarcely recognise the interior if he could see it to-day.

The country changed and became quite different after leaving Stockton. It is curious how unlike County Durham is to Yorkshire.

At Sedgefield we turned left, and after about four miles

Burn Hall, Durham.

came on to the Great North Road at Bushyford. We passed through several mining villages where crowds of unemployed men and lads stared at the horses with eager interest written all over their pale faces.

Just beyond the bridge over the Wear at Croxdale we found ourselves at the lodge gates of Burn Hall. It needed a good deal of explanation before the lodgekeeper would open them and allow the caravan into the drive. She had her suspicions that, in spite of the fact that I told her we were expected, we were merely a couple of gipsies.

The mansion of Burn Hall, built in the Classical style of architecture, formerly owned by a branch of the Salvin family, was bought by St. Joseph's Foreign Missionary Society in 1926. They have adapted it as a college for a section of their students. The Society was founded by Cardinal Vaughan in 1866 with the object of providing priests for work on the foreign missions. The members are more often referred to as the ' Mill Hill Missionaries ' as their mother house is at Mill Hill, a northern suburb of London.

The Superior welcomed us most hospitably, and I enjoyed some interesting talks with the professors and students, who while strolling about the grounds in their black cassocks and broad scarlet cinctures seemed very curious to have a look inside the wagon.

In addition to a sketch of Burn Hall I also had time to draw the interior of the chapel at Croxdale Hall, about a mile away. This has been the home of the Salvins for many centuries, for they are one of the oldest Catholic families in the north of England. It is probable that Mass has been said at Croxdale since the 15th century, or even earlier. The present chapel is of no great interest from the point of view of architecture, having been erected about a hundred years ago in the so-called ' Strawberry Hill ' style of Gothic.

Opposite the Hall is a pre-Reformation chapel, used for Protestant worship at one time, but which came back into Catholic hands when the Lord of the Manor built a new parish

St. Hubert's, Croxdale.

church in the village for his Anglican tenants.

I could not help feeling surprised to find that this ancient building had been allowed to fall into such a sad state of disrepair and to hear that Mass is not said within these walls which date from soon after the Norman Conquest.

Leaving Burn Hall early yesterday afternoon we had no more than five or six miles to do before we reached Ushaw College. There was a long hill to climb, but Jack and Bill made nothing of it, although with the heavy load of the old van they would have scarcely managed such an ascent.

The procurator had made all arrangements for us to leave the caravan at the college farm. For Ushaw not only boasts its own big farm, but also its private coal-mine and post office. We have seldom been treated with such generous hospitality. In fact it would seem that whatever we need can be had for the asking—and nothing to pay—whether it is corn for the horses, or milk, butter and eggs for my larder.

Here is a sketch which I made during High Mass this Sunday morning, which gives an idea of the interior of St. Cuthbert's Chapel, the largest of the several chapels which are to be found within the vast precincts of the college.

Neither Tony nor myself will forget this week-end in a hurry. All the professors have gone out of their way to make us feel at home and to show us the many interesting features of this great establishment. Nor must the college farmer and his large family be forgotten, for they have taken a pride in looking after Jack and Bill.

There is no place in England which can be compared with Ushaw. It is unique. Like St. Edmund's College, Ware, already mentioned in an earlier chapter, St. Cuthbert's, Ushaw, can claim to have been founded at Douai in Flanders by Cardinal Allen in 1568. The French Revolution forced the professors and students to seek refuge in England. Some settled at Old Hall, Ware; others found a home at Tudhoe, near Durham, whence they moved to Pontop Hall, near Lan-

St. Cuthbert's College, Ushaw.

chester, then to Crook Hall, before finally establishing themselves at Ushaw. The oldest portion of the vast group of buildings, which form a prominent landmark for many miles, was opened in 1808. Since then the story of Ushaw College has been one of continuous growth and expansion. It provides educational facilities for both clerical and lay students.

Even with a good bump of locality on which I pride myself I admit that I found it hard to find my way about, so complicated are the many passages and corridors which link up the various sections of the college buildings. Many architects have had a share in designing them, including the three Pugins and the two Hansoms. St. Cuthbert's Chapel, which I have sketched, was built in 1883 during the presidency of Mgr. Wrennall.

Our stay has not been nearly long enough to allow us to examine all the treasures of the museum, library, and sacristy. I enjoyed the inspiring vigour and lustiness of the singing at High Mass. The plain chant may lack the polish and refinement of the monks of Solesmes, but it possesses a virile beauty of its own, which seems to be in keeping with the grey stone walls, the bleak windswept moorlands and the whole spirit of Northumbria. Even more inspiring were the English hymns at May Devotions on Saturday night, which can only be compared to the roar of the sea breaking on a rocky shore.

Sitting up on the screen between the anti-chapel and the choir I gazed down on the stalls. I pictured all the generations of students who had passed through Ushaw, and who had distinguished themselves in almost every walk of life—more than 1,000 priests, nearly 40 bishops, 5 archbishops, and 4 cardinals were students here at one time. Statesmen, soldiers, sailors, artists, judges, and authors—you will find every profession represented on the roll of famous alumni.

Ushaw gives one the feeling of being able to retain a happy combination of hoary old age and perennial youth. But it is time I went to bed for we have to be up early to-morrow.

I resisted the temptation to sketch the Cathedral when passing through Durham after leaving Ushaw, devoting the time instead to the not very interesting exterior of St. Cuthbert's Catholic Church, whose eventful history is worth recording.

There always seems to have been a priest living in hiding at Durham throughout the Penal Days. It is stated that Bishop Leyburn confirmed as many as 1,024 persons here in 1687; enough to prove that the people of Durham had remained loyal to the Old Religion even if the great minster where pilgrims used to flock to the shrines of St. Cuthbert and St. Bede had been desecrated by Protestants. A new chapel was built here in 1827, and still remains in use to-day, although much altered. A precious relic can be venerated in this church—the hand of the Venerable Nicholas Postgate, the Yorkshire martyr, whom I mentioned in my description of Ugthorpe.

Onward by the Great North Road and never had we met with such continuous traffic. Skirting Chester-le-Street by the by-pass which avoids the town, we reached Birtley, where St. Joseph's Catholic Church stands on the main street. I made a rapid sketch of the exterior while a group of miners gazed with curiosity and interest at the unusual sight of a real live artist at work on the pavement.

Jesuit missionaries kept alive the Faith in this part of the country from about the latter half of the 17th century. Later on they were succeeded by Benedictines who have been here for over a hundred years. The present church dates from 1842 and was enlarged in 1862. It is in no way remarkable, but struck me as being cared for with more than usual attention—indeed just what one ought to find in a Benedictine church.

The sketch being finished I looked for the caravan. But it had disappeared. I hurried on and after about ten minutes walk, beheld its familiar shape about quarter of a mile ahead of me, steadily climbing a long hill. Eventually, feeling very hot and cross, I managed to overtake it A mean trick on the part of my companion! I climbed aboard and sat down for a rest. But not for long, for within a mile or so we suddenly

St. Cuthbert's, Durham.

started bumping and rattling over cobbles which continued without any relief until we were past Newcastle. I got off and walked, and I fear that Tony must have felt very sore after such a painful ordeal.

Through Gateshead and across the new bridge over the Tyne. How people stared at our caravan! You might have supposed they had never seen the like before. Negotiating trams and buses, my companion drove on across the Town Moor until at last we reached our destination—the Convent of the Good Shepherd, South Gosforth, where the Mother Prioress had promised to provide a field for the horses. The van itself rested in a yard behind the convent.

There are no less than fourteen Catholic churches in Newcastle. I made sketches of two of them; St. Andrew's, Worswick Street, and St. Mary's Cathedral.

The former is the oldest in the city. There was a ' Popish Mass House ' not far from the site of the present church in the reign of James II, followed by other chapels which were eventually replaced by the modern St. Andrew's, built in 1875. It is not a beautiful church by any means, but it gives the impression of being very much alive. Seldom do you find yourself alone, for all day long people are coming and going. It may well be described as a ' House of Prayer.'

St. Mary's Cathedral occupies a central position close to the railway station; the lofty spire being very conspicuous. It was opened in 1844—the event being marked out for the holding of a great Catholic demonstration at which eight bishops were present. The church was designed by Augustus Welby Pugin and is quite typical of his genius. But unfortunately the effect of the interior has been much spoilt by subsequent decorations, and by the insertion of skylights in the roof. The master's criticisms, if he were alive to-day, might be considered too outspoken for publication in some of our Catholic papers! But one is glad to record that his stone rood screen has not been removed as in Southwark Cathedral and elsewhere. One can

St. Andrew's, Newcastle-on-Tyne.

only hope that sooner or later this beautiful specimen of the Gothic revival will be redecorated by someone who understands and appreciates the work of the elder Pugin.

After two days at the Good Shepherd Convent we got away and continued our journey northwards. I was sitting within the van, busily employed in cleaning the Primus stove, when suddenly there was a violent bump and I found myself on the floor which had shot up at an alarming angle. I put my head out of the door and asked what had happened.

" Wheel off ! " remarked Tony. He clambered off his seat on to the road, and I followed him.

" Get hold of the horses heads, or they may bolt," he said.

A crowd of miners collected from all sides and stood by watching us.

" Ah, she'll tak' some hoistin'," remarked one of them.

Tony asked where there was a blacksmith or joiner and went off to find them. I was left with the horses, who had been got out of the shafts by this time. They stood side by side on the path, looking rather puzzled at what had happened. Jack contemplated a privet hedge the other side of the fence—but wisely decided it wasn't worth eating. Bill indulged in profound meditation.

Some of the miners started to mess about with the van; trying to hoist it up, but with no success. Tony came back after awhile having borrowed a jack.

With much heaving and vocal accompaniment on the part of the miners—the crowd had now increased to such numbers that the traffic on the Great North Road was being held up—the van was got into position and the missing wheel fitted on. But this was merely a makeshift job until we could reach the smithy.

The horses were put back into the shafts and with great care Tony started off again—hoping that the wheel would hold on until we got to the blacksmith's. We managed to do so and remained there about an hour while the wheel was repaired.

Having eaten our midday meal we continued the journey, and reached Morpeth.

Here I discovered the little church of St. Robert on the banks of the Wansbeck, which provided me with a charming composition to sketch. This "neat and commodious Gothic structure" (as a contemporary writer described it on the opening ceremony in 1849) has been served by monks of the English Benedictine congregation for over a century. It replaced a chapel in Oldgate, dedicated to St. Bede, which had been used by Catholics in this district since 1778.

We left Morpeth behind us and started to climb. As the road ascended the long range of the Cheviots appeared far away to the north. We were now in sight of the Scottish Border. Farming country, now mostly given over for grazing purposes, with young lambs skipping about in the fields. Long rows of tall unclipped hawthorn that scarcely deserve to be called hedges divide off these fields—such are the main features of the Northumbrian landscape.

We climbed up on to a high plateau, nearly 500 feet above sea level, and about three miles ahead of us was the village of Longhorsley for which we had been making.

"Stronghorsely," my companion remarked would be a better title, and more in keeping with the hilly trail we had been following since leaving Morpeth. Down we went until we reached the village of solid and well built stone houses.

The Catholic church of St. Thomas of Canterbury was easy to locate. It stands right in the centre of the village. Here we found Fr. James Wright who had been expecting us all the afternoon. We explained the reason of our delay on the road as he took us to the field where the horses were to graze. He told us to leave the caravan in the drive of the presbytery where we enjoyed his hospitality for the next two days, not forgetting the rare privilege of a good hot bath.

The district round Longhorsley remained Catholic long after the Reformation, but in recent years the congregation has

P.F.A. 9.5.1934

St. Robert's, Morpeth.

become greatly reduced, mainly through the disappearance of so many Catholic landowning families.

There is an ancient Peel Tower, formerly belonging to the Horsley family. In 1853 it was converted into a Catholic chapel and presbytery. During the 18th century this remote and lonely mission was usually served by the Society of Jesus. In 1843 the existing Gothic church was built; in place of the old chapel within the Peel Tower. A few years ago the diocesan authorities decided to sell the latter and to-day the priest occupies a modern house whose startling red brick walls are a violent contrast to the worn grey stones of the old Tower and church. Maybe the architect felt he must try to do his bit to liven up Longhorsley!

We spent the greater part of Ascension day in this peaceful Northumbrian village, Tony occupying some hours in giving the wheel a thorough clean and oiling. We resumed our journey between 3 and 4 o'clock. Owing to Jack's habitual restiveness we nearly collided with the gate post in getting out of the drive. But Tony has now learnt that a bit of whip cord makes him think twice before starting to play tricks.

It was quite hot that afternoon; the first taste of summer weather we had enjoyed since leaving Yorkshire. There was a long descent into the Vale of Coquet. We left the main road at the bridge over the river, and turned left up the valley along a narrow lane that twisted and turned, and whose steep ' banks ' gave the horses little chance to take things easy.

We passed through Rothbury and about three miles beyond arrived at the smaller village of Tropton, where we met the congregation leaving the church after Benediction.

The horses were sodden with sweat after their hot pull. How they enjoyed a drink in the river! Just as at Longhorsley, so here in Thropton we were given a royal welcome by the priest. Fr. Goundry may be sure neither of us have forgotten his kindness to us—not to mention the special cider which was opened when he entertained us to dinner. The caravan stood in a farmyard just opposite the church. The

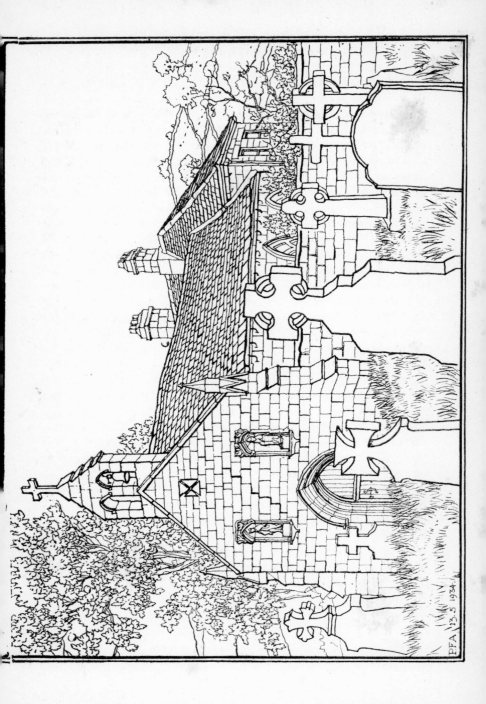

All Saints, Thropton.

horses grazed in the presbytery meadow.

Thropton is one of the oldest Catholic missions in Northumberland, founded about 1700. But for some reason or other there are few records of its early history. The original chapel at Thropton Hall, the home of the Robson family, was pulled down in 1811. It was mainly through the generosity of this family that the present church was built in 1811—a typical North of England ' Popish Mass House ' of the pre-Emancipation times. Severe and plain without, the interior is in startling contrast, being brightly decorated. The style of architecture might be termed " very early Gothic Revival." One can see from the loving care bestowed on this venerable shrine, that Fr. Goundry appreciates and values it. On the old tombstones in the churchyard you can read the names of many an old family which helped to keep alive the Faith in Northumberland during the centuries of persecution.

One day during our stay at Thropton we were taken to Biddlestone Hall—up among the Cheviots. Thanks to the Selby family the Old Religion never died out in this wild and remote district. Mass has been said at Biddlestone Hall without a break for over 600 years, for somehow or other it was generally possible to keep a priest here. Sad to relate the estates were sold to Protestants some years ago, but it is good to know that the present owners allow the chapel to remain in use for Catholic worship.

We were shown over the place by Fr. Francis Hutchinson, now in charge of the mission of Biddlestone. He explained to us that the chapel was built on the upper floor of an old Peel Tower, and is therefore not so lofty as might be supposed from my sketch of the ivy covered exterior. A sad place in some ways, but a forceful reminder of what was the price paid by our forefathers for their loyalty to Catholicism.

PFA. 12. 5. 1934.

Biddlestone Hall.

EIGHT

Whittingham—Lowick—Berwick-on-Tweed—across the Border Grantshouse—Dunbar—Drum-Mohr, Leavenhall— Edinburgh.

As will be realised we have had a busy week since leaving Ushaw. Apart from the accident to the wheel just after setting off from Newcastle, nothing very startling has occurred, and I have been able to devote myself to the chief object of this pilgrimage, i.e., sketching churches. To-morrow we shall be leaving Thropton, and by the time I continue this travel-diary I hope we shall have reached Edinburgh.

It rained hard all the eight miles or so that we covered between Thropton and Whittingham, our next stopping place. We arrived there rather cold and wet, but were soon cheered up by the affectionate welcome given us by that kind old priest, Father Charles Hart, who, despite his white hair, still retains the spirit and vitality of a youthful school-boy. I feel sure he will not object to this comparison—most of his life having been spent in teaching at St. Cuthbert's Grammar School, Newcastle, where many of the younger generation of the priests of the Hexham and Newcastle diocese were among his pupils.

He insisted on the caravan being left in the drive in front of his church and took us round his lovely garden, which is also a bird sanctuary, where he has built a Lourdes grotto, likewise a striking Calvary which appears in my sketch. We joined him in saying the Rosary that night in the little Romanesque church which stands in the midst of this peaceful garden. It was erected in 1876 by Sir Henry and Lady Beding-field; replacing the old chapel at Callaly Castle, the mansion of the Clavering family. Ever since the Reformation this branch of the Clavering's had been among the most stalwart defenders

St. Mary's, Whittingham.

of Catholicism in Northumberland, and it is sad to find that the property has changed hands, and that the Catholic population around here is so reduced in numbers. Many of the fittings and priceless old vestments that belonged to Callaly Castle are now at Whittingham. Few country parishes possess such treasures.

It continued to rain nearly all the way from Whittingham to Wooler, a distance of about twelve miles which we covered during the forenoon. On the left lay the Cheviots; on the right farm land, nearly all under grass, for sheep are the chief concern of the farmers in this part of Northumberland. Wooler is an old market town where the Catholic Religion managed to retain its hold throughout the 17th and 18th centuries, although there was not a permanent chapel in the town before 1843. It was a very humble affair, built over a malt kiln. A mission house was erected in 1843, but destroyed by fire ten years later. The present church, a well proportioned building in the Early English style of Gothic was opened in 1859. The interior is rather cold and dreary and deserves careful redecoration.

From Wooler we took the road for Berwick-on-Tweed. Looking back as the horses pulled the van up on to Doddington Moor there were glorious views of the rolling Cheviots. Far away to the right was the North Sea.

A few miles to our left, hidden away in the heart of the Cheviots, lies the village of Yetholm. I wished we had not been pressed for time, for I had often wanted to visit Yetholm, since it was the headquarters of the gipsies in Lowland Scotland for more than two centuries. From the Cheviots they often wandered down into Northumberland, and even as far south as Durham and Yorkshire. The most celebrated of all the tribes which frequented Yetholm was that of the Faas, whose chief claimed descent from the " Earl of Little Egypt." In the 17th century, one of this tribe, William Faa, was treated as a king by his subjects, as one learns from an article in *Blackwood's Magazine,* quoted by Mr. Simson in his *History of the Gipsies.* " On solemn occasions," so we are told, " William Faa assumed all the stately deportment of sovereignty. He had twenty-four children, and at each of their christenings he appeared, dressed in his original wedding-robes. Twenty young handmaidens were always present, as part of the family retinue, and for the purpose of waiting on the numerous guests. Besides Will's gipsy associates, several of the neighbouring farmers and lairds, with whom he was on terms of friendly intercourse, used to attend these christenings."

We passed a farm training school for boys. Some of the lads stopped us on the road and asked for a match; then gaining confidence demanded a " fag." They got both. " We work here " they informed us, " learning to farm, but we don't like it ! " From what we gathered it seemed to be an " Approved School," similar to St. William's, Market Weighton.

About 7 o'clock we drove into Lowick where Fr. Thompson told us we could put the van into a small yard next the church. There was plenty of grass in the yard, despite its limited space. Rather than walk a mile or so to a farm we decided to leave the horses there for the night. The cottage adjoining the yard was occupied by a lady tenant who became enthusiastic over Jack and Bill. "What grand beasts they are ! " she murmured. " I *am* glad you are staying in here."

Tony and I went to bed and fell asleep to the sound of the horses munching away beside the van. About midnight we were suddenly awakened by a piercing scream. It came from the unfortunate Bill, whom Jack had been biting for getting in his way. Bill could never defend himself. Tony got out of bed, put on his trousers, and having secured Jack, tied him up to an old door beneath the cottage, leaving Bill to wander where he chose. When we met the lady of the cottage she remarked to us with less enthusiasm than the previous evening " What a horrible row those horses made. I couldn't sleep a wink."

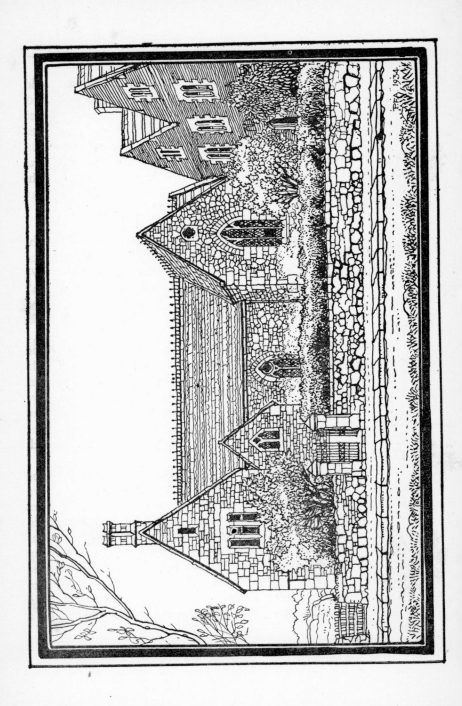

St. Edward the Confessor, Lowick.

The mission of Lowick dates from 1861 and was first served from Wooler. The little church which I have sketched, contains many interesting fittings; pictures, statues, vestments, etc., which formerly belonged to the chapel at Haggerston Castle, formerly the chief residence of the old Catholic family of Haggerston, to whom the preservation of the Faith in this part of Northumberland is mainly due. They were always loyal adherents to the Stuart cause. The Castle has now been pulled down. Fr. Thompson told us that as in all the other country missions we had visited in Northumberland, the number of Catholics has greatly diminished in recent years. We could understand how different is the work of a priest in these rural districts.

After breakfasting with Fr. Thompson we left Lowick and started off to cover the few remaining miles on English soil. About two hours later our caravan was rumbling over the new bridge across the Tweed and entered Berwick. Here I discovered the little church of Our Lady and St. Cuthbert hidden away in a back street close to the town walls with which Berwick is still partly surrounded.

During the 17th century Jesuit missionaries came here from time to time, but little record has been preserved of their labours. Later on the mission was served by Benedictines. The first chapel was built in 1829. It was replaced in 1846 by the present building erected by the Rev. Thomas Witham.

The caravan attached a vast amount of interest among the children who seemed to have gathered around it from every quarter of the Border Town. Just as we were starting our dinner, a policeman asked us to move. I clung on to the kettle, coffee pots and plates, while Tony drove off over the bumpy cobbles. Having reached the spot indicated by the policeman we resumed our meal.

We started off again, having washed up, but soon found ourselves at the tail end of a long funeral procession, following about thirty cars, crawling along at a snail's pace in the direction of the cemetery.

At last we got away from them and approached the Border. " Fine day! " remarked a roadman to Tony.

I thought it my duty to explain to him that a remark about the state of the weather was the usual greeting in Scotland, and that if he hailed folk with his usual Yorkshire " How are you? " they would be somewhat mystified at this enquiry after their health.

We passed the last farm in England where the most recent addition to the population—a skewbald foal—was suckling its mother. Another half mile we reached " The First Public House in Scotland." I took a photograph of the caravan and horses behind which was a sign post on whose two arms are the words " *England—Scotland.*" No customs examination or producing of passports is needed at this strange frontier post. But will it always be so? Who can say? Perhaps those two words " *England—Scotland* " may yet have a more real significance than they do at present.

My companion was much interested at the first " But and Ben " we passed; the characteristic Scottish cottage, two storied but low, a window at each side, a door in the middle, and two small skylights in the roof. He noticed too how the " look " of the country had changed within half an hour; how the small farms of England had given place to great farms whose buildings were almost a self-contained village. Rising above nearly all of them was a tall chimney.

" What's it for? " he asked me. " Is it where they cook the Scotch broth or distill the whisky?"

He was also much intrigued at the bevy of young lassies who were sorting potatoes in a field beside the road; especially at their uniform costume—black skirts, strong boots, a sack tied round their waists, and the wide brimmed hats. Even more fascinated was he by another group of elderly women whose hats were of a different colour and pattern. Then there were the Clydesdale horses, sometimes as many as six teams at work in a field; all fine, big, well fed and groomed beasts, whose gear was heavily adorned with shining brass or nickle-plated "jewellry," which flashed in the sunlight; clashing, tinkling, and creaking as the horses strode along, with tossing heads.

He remarked to me that the farmers must take a real pride in such chargers; so different to the majority of teams in the South.

We looked down on the roofs of the fishing village of Burnmouth, passed through Ayton, and about 7.30 managed to find camping ground near Grantshouse Station. We had done more than 22 miles since leaving Lowick that morning.

We were up soon after 5 a.m. and there was no sign of life as we drove away from Grantshouse. Moreover at this early hour we had the road to ourselves; a rare treat.

By Cockburnspath and along the sea-shore, we reached Dunbar where I made a rapid sketch of the little church of Our Lady of the Waves; the first Catholic place of worship we had come across since leaving England. Somehow or other this little church seemed to express the status of Catholicism in the social life of modern Scotland.

While wandering through the streets of Dunbar I wondered if the house is still standing which belonged to the gipsy family of Faa, which has already been mentioned a few pages back. One of the Faas became a rich merchant of Dunbar about 1670, and in 1734 Captain James Fall (the family name having been changed to Fall), was elected member of Parliament for Dunbar. His descendants figured many times as provosts and baillies of this ancient burgh. What is more they were proud of their gipsy origin. One of them went so far as to have the history of the Faas depicted on an elaborate tapestry which adorned his house. Even when they became merchants and adopted a civilised life, they seem to have retained much of their gipsy temperament, for it was the same blood that ran in their veins as that of John Faa, who in 1643 was bold enough to carry off the wife of the Earl of Cassilis, during the absence of this noble lord from home. Later on when one of the Dunbar Falls married Sir John Anstruther of Elie, his relatives took no pains to show their disapproval of his wife's gipsy origin.

We stopped for dinner on the new by pass road at East Linton where the levels of the clover and grass on either side provided a satisfactory free meal for Jack and Bill.

Moving on again we made another halt outside Haddington where I wanted to sketch the St. Mary's Church, a small gothic building erected in 1862 to provide for the spiritual needs of the Irish farm labourers who by that date had settled in thousands all over the Lothians. There we had tea and once more resumed our journey. The horses began to get tired and Tony had to force them a bit.

This was their second long day on the roads. Tranent seemed very far away and the milestones further and further apart as the pace got slower. As we passed through this mining village everybody turned round to stare at the brown caravan and horses. We arrived at the brow of a hill, and right ahead of us Arthur's Seat stood up against the setting sun; a welcome sight. Then a long descent for some miles until at last we got down to Leavenhall where once again the van began to creak and shake as it passed over cobble stones. A sharp turn to the right along by the sea shore, then through a lodge gates and a wooded drive — Drum-Mohr — the new monastery of the Passionist Fathers whose superior had told us we should be welcome there.

Bill seemed to know he had reached the end of a thirty-four mile pull, for he suddenly took on a new lease of life after passing the lodge, and trotted up the drive.

The sons of St. Paul of the Cross in their black habits with the badge of the Passion on their breasts, came out to welcome us. We unyoked the horses, helped by one of the Brothers whose home was on a farm away in Ireland and who seemed

St. Francis', Lothian Street, Edinburgh.

to know all about horses. Very tired and weary we soon fell asleep that night.

The Passionists made their first foundation in Scotland in 1859 when they took over St. Mungo's parish, near the old pre-Reformation Cathedral in Glasgow. During the past seventy years they have also done great work as missioners all over the country. They were invited to settle in the archdiocese of St. Andrew's and Edinburgh by the present Archbishop and rented the large property of Drum-Mohr which became the "Retreat of Our Lady Immaculate." Here the community chiefly consists of students. There is a public chapel adjoining the mansion which supplies the needs of Catholics in the surrounding district.

We remained at Drum-Mohr for three days, during which I was fully occupied making drawings of some of the Catholic churches of Edinburgh. Tony explored the city on his own and thought it a much better sort of place than London.

Here is a sketch of the new church of S.S. Ninian and Triduana, in the eastern suburb of Restalrig. Not far off once stood a holy well and collegiate church dedicated to St. Triduana who founded a Nunnery here. Both the church and convent were destroyed by the Reformers as "monuments of idolatry." Thanks to the zeal of the present rector, Mgt. Miley, a new church is being erected here, designed by Sir Giles Gilbert Scott. When completed it wil! be one of the most striking buildings in or around Edinburgh.

NINE

Edinburgh—Colinton—Linlithgow—Polmont—Stirling—
Dunblane—Auchterarder—Perth—St. Mary's, Kinnoull.

It was very early when we left Drum-Mohr, for I hoped to
get as far as Stirling by the end of the day, or at any rate
within a few miles of it. Edinburgh's cobbled streets and
traffic signs had better be avoided. So I pored over the map,
wondering which would be our best route. I was not very
familiar with the rapidly growing suburbs on the south of the
city.

It was certainly a winding and twisting route. I had to be
ready to shout out to Tony " Turn right! " " Turn left " as
the occasion demanded. We passed many small collieries—
people often forget that there is quite an extensive " Black
Country " within a few miles of Princes Street. Maybe genteel
Edinburgh residents prefer to ignore this blot on the landscape?

Then on through the big new housing estate of Niddrie
Mains—where some of Edinburgh's slum-clearance population
have been dumped.

Arthur's Seat disappeared behind us, and the long range
of the Pentlands came into view on reaching Liberton. Here
we stopped for a breakfast outside the Poor Clare Convent.

After an hour or more the caravan descended a steep hill
into Colinton. Here we did some shopping. The grocer
wanted to know where we came from. He knew Yorkshire
quite well, so asked many questions about our journey.

It seems that we ought to have noticed the Covenanters
Monument—" Did ye nae see it? " enquired the grocer, " Aye!
There's folk who come here from all parts of the world just
to look at yon monument."

St. Ninian's, Restalrig.

Tony only having been taught English history at school had never heard of the Covenanters. So I had to explain to him, after we left Colinton, that they were very important people in Scotland's troubled history. But he didn't seem very interested, having no use for the squabbles of the various species of Prostestants in byegone ages.

A succession of narrow lanes which twisted and turned finally brought us out onto the main Edinburgh-Stirling road. We lunched by a canal bridge where we unloosed the horses to graze by the roadside.

The landscape is now dominated by the lofty pink slag heaps which are piled up round the shale oil mines. Some of them, especially those near Winchburgh, are really most impressive. I wonder why no artist has not been inspired to draw or paint them? They possess a sort of grim beauty of colour and form, certainly when seen at dawn or sunset.

We meet the first lot of tinkers—a man and a handsome young woman, both pulling a cart, laden up with a tent, old cans, and bits of tin. Their clothes are worn and shabby, but seem to be chosen with care and discrimination as to what would suit them best. How is it that the gipsies and tinkers, at least the genuine sort, know instinctively how to " dress well "? Where do they pick up those black felt hats, always bent to just the right shape, and those scarves of vivid colour? Are there tailors hidden away in town who possess a tradition of fitting the particular kind of suit? I have often wished to find out.

We hail our fellow vagrants and get a friendly greeting in return. Leaving the shale mines behind us we move on through farming country reminding us of what we had seen in East Lothian.

The country which we were now passing through used to be one of the chief headquarters of gipsies and tinkers about a century ago, and even to-day one comes across a good many of these vagrants round Linlithgow and Falkirk. The probable reason for the selection of this part of the country was its then populous character, and that all the traffic between Glasgow and Edinburgh passed within a few miles of the spot near Linlithgow, where was their largest camp. It also lay fairly close to the main road between the north of Scotland and England. So, as the caravan creaked and rattled along this road, I felt that we had arrived in a friendly environment, and where our presence would not evoke such surprise as elsewhere. But whether we should have been welcomed as friends by the McDonalds, Jamiesons, Wilsons, Gordons, and Lundies, who about 1850 did good business as tinsmiths, horn-spoons, or in horse-dealing, is another matter. Quite possibly they would have regarded us as intruders on their domains and preserves.

The inhabitants of Linlithgow found it wiser to be on good terms with the "tinklers," and the magistrates of this royal burgh stood in awe of them, seldom daring to convict them when brought up for trial on a charge of theft. One is told that " the more respectable inhabitants of Linlithgowshire deigned to play at golf and other games with the principle members of the body," who were proficient at all kinds of sport, not to mention dancing. Mr. Simson informs us that " the honourable magistrates indeed, frequently admitted the presumptuous tinklers to share a social bowl with them at their entertainments and dinner parties " despite the fact that the tinklers had their usual homes either in tents or on the ground floor of half-ruined houses, without furniture, save a few blankets and straw.

They were a bold and irrepressible crowd, these Linlithgowshire gipsies of a hundred years ago—the men folk exceptionally handsome often elegantly dressed in the height of fashion. Of one of the McDonalds it is told that he was frequently observed in three or four different costumes in one market-day. Then on another occasion he would be met in a ragged coat, with a pack on his back—just a typical vagrant " tinkler." It would need a volume in which to recount their exploits—the bold robberies they managed to carry off, the sheep stealings, and the murders. They regarded the rich as their lawful prey, but they were always good friends to the poor—as ready to give away a purse of money as to take it; living according to a code of honour peculiar to themselves, more akin to the savage tribes of Central Asia than to the conventional morality of 18th and 19th century Scotland, against which they were always in open revolt.

The caravan created quite a stir as it rumbled and jolted over the cobble stones of the long main street of Linlithgow. Doors opened and heads peered out. " Look! Here's a tinker's van. Aye! Yon's a bonnie pair of horses! "

I left Tony to get tea ready, telling him I would be back again before the kettle had boiled, and went off to visit the Catholic Church which I found to be one of Peter Paul Pugin's characteristic designs in Decorated English Gothic. Linlithgow still retains its glorious pre-Reformation kirk, but no trace remains of its twenty-nine altars. John Knox and his rabble took good care to destroy them, as well as the adjacent Dominican and Carmelite friaries. So thoroughly was Linlithgow purged of Popery that there is no record of Mass having been said here again for nearly three hundred years.

But the industrial development of West Lothian in the early part of the last century induced large colonies of Irish to settle in this district. By 1850 they were reckoned to number over a thousand. Except when visited by a priest from Edinburgh at rare intervals they had no opportunity to practice their religion. It must have needed immense faith and courage on the part of the Rev. Francis Mackerrell to accept the charge of these Irish Catholics when appointed here in 1851. His mission included Bathgate and Bo'ness as well as Linlithgow. So great was the bigotry of the local Prostestants that he had to wait six years before he could secure a chapel. Eventually he managed to buy a disused Presbyterian Kirk which was adapted for Catholic worship. And this is how the Faith returned to Linlithgow. The present church was built in 1888.

Tea was waiting for me when I got back to the van. Tony

St. Michael's, Linlithgow.

had been examining the curious old fountain with its quaint inscription, " St. Michael is kinde to strangers." He remarked to me that he hoped the Archangel would be " kinde " to us.

My companion was also interested in the big farms which are such a feature round Linlithgow. He could not get over the size of them as compared with those in his native Yorkshire. It was good to discover there were certain things in this foreign land which he thought worthy to be praised.

We pass one of the strangest objects which we have yet come across. From the back view we cannot decide if it is a man or woman. Great heavy boots project beneath a long coat of which must have been dark blue in colour, but which is now faded to a dull greenish grey. On getting nearer we detect a black skirt—so we discover the sex of its wearer. Her back is bent and she toils along wearily. As we pass by we get a closer look—a queer old face, red and wrinkled—with such tired eyes. We give her a friendly greeting. But there is no response. She never even turns her head in our direction. Who is this strange wanderer, and what is her history? What is she brooding over as she drags herself along the road.

Then in startling contrast a smart little scarlet sports car flashes past, driven by a bright young thing whose red lips are even more vivid than the paint work on her car. Unlike the other woman she looks our way. Perhaps she would like to exchange her car for our caravan?

About 7 o'clock we reach the village of Polmont. Both driver and horses are tired, for we have been on the road for over twelve hours. Tony and I decide that it is better to stop here and not proceed any further.

I enquire at a joiner's where we can find a camp site. A certain farm is suggested. So I go off to look for it. There is some difficulty in persuading the farmer to let us stop, and before meeting him I had to interview his daughter. The grazing might be better, for sheep have already eaten up most of the grass. Still it is a nice quiet spot and we spend a restful evening; Tony polishing harness while we listen to the wireless.

The next morning I had a nasty shock when asking what we had to pay for the night. "Four shillings" said the farmer. Of course I ought to have bargained beforehand, but it never occured to me that farmers in West Lothian would be so grasping. In all our experiences of farmers neither before or since were we asked to pay so much, the invariable price demanded being 2/- or 1/6 a night, Tony discovered later on that he had left his favourite knife behind. He had to buy a new one, so we reckoned that Polmont had cost us at least 7/-!

We got away about 7 a.m. Jack chose to be a nuisance, rearing up in the shafts, just as Tony had harnessed him. It was a lovely morning with bright sunshine, and we soon forgot about our expensive night's lodging.

After a couple of hours we stopped for breakfast. Tony, noticing a pond beside the road, took a bucket to water the horses. A woman stepped out from a cottage and called to him "Yon's nae guid for horses. It's a cess pool! There's a tap here!" So he turned back and filled his bucket at the tap.

Grangemouth, with the masts and funnels of ships, rising up above the houses, and timber yards lay to our right. Beyond it the long range of the Ochil Hills across the Forth.

The road was almost dead level for the next four or five miles, so we made good progress until we reached the outskirts of Stirling. I took care to point out Wallace's monument to Tony, not forgetting to remind him that only a mile or so to our left his fellow countrymen suffered a bad defeat from Robert Bruce's little band of pikemen just over six centuries ago. But he was too absorbed in negotiating the traffic to be greatly interested in my history lesson.

For it was market day, and even at normal times the narrow streets of Stirling are not exactly suitable for a gipsy caravan.

St. Mary's, Stirling.

I was glad I was walking and not inside the van, for the cobble stones seemed to be harder and more bumpy than usual. Tony had to grin and bear them.

At length I told him to stop as it was necessary to buy something for our lunch, the larder being empty. I also wished to make a sketch of the Catholic Church, which I found without having to ask the way, for Peter Paul Pugin's red sandstone "English Decorated Gothic" betrays the presence of Popery no matter how many other places of worship may surround it. In Stirling the architect took advantage of the site at his disposal and the approach from the steep street is quite impressive. But what a poor substitute for the pre-Reformation Greyfriar's Kirk, is this modern church. For one thing the former is so definitely "Scottish" in feeling and inspiration, whereas the latter is merely an exotic excrescence which would do just as well in Stockport or Stoke-on-Trent as in Stirling.

For nearly three centuries the " gray bulwark of the North " remained without a Catholic church for Protestantism triumphed in this burgh at the Reformation. It was due to the Irish immigrants that the Faith returned to Stirling. So numerous were they by 1838 that the Rev. Paul McLachlan, then in charge of a newly opened mission at Lennoxstown, erected what a contemporary journalist described as a "neat Gothic Chapel and house." The building was enlarged in 1850 when, so we are told, "Miss Malony and the choir performed Haydn No. 1." I wonder what the composer would have thought of this rendering of his music? Anyhow I don't suppose the congregation was critical, and I'm sure Miss Malony and her choir felt very proud of their ambitious effort. The "neat Gothic chapel" was in use until 1904 when it was replaced by the existing church, the cost of which was defrayed by Mrs. Murray of Polmaise, a generous benefactress to Scottish Catholicism.

Having completed my sketch I walked back to the caravan. Then we drove on across the bridge over the Forth, and so northwards. Just after passing Causewayhead we stopped for our mid-day meal, giving Jack and Bill a feed of corn as there was no grass to be had.

The passing of a gipsy caravan through Bridge of Allen's main street created quite a sensation. I felt we did not ' fit in ' with those genteel villas in their prim little gardens. Still the inhabitants were very interested. They came out and stared hard at this evidently rare spectacle for which no charge was made.

I told Tony that Bridge of Allen is a select holiday resort, explaining that people come here to drink the waters. " What for? " he enquired. " ' Constipation and skin diseases '—at least this is what the guide book says."

I wished there had been time to stop outside the gates of Keir House as I should like to have examined the Byzantine chapel, erected by the late Brigadier-General Archibald Stirling, which I had often admired in photographs. For the same reason I did not make a sketch of Reginald Fairlie's delightful new church at Dunblane which we passed on the outskirts of the old town. I paid a hasty visit to the cathedral and to a baker's shop; returning to the caravan with a good supply of scones, ' soft biscuits ' and ' cookies ' which Tony enjoyed for his tea.

We cover another eight miles or so. About 6.30 it seems clear that the horses have done enough for one day—Jack is very weary. An R.A.C. scout whom we meet at Greenloaning cross-roads advises me to try the neighbouring pub for a field. I find the landlord and everything is soon arranged. The horses have a good feed, while Tony spends the time between supper and bed time in cleaning harness.

We are now in Perthshire—" the fairest portion of the Northern Kingdom " as Sir Walter Scott described it. Our route lies through rich and fertile country, big fields of oats, barley and potatoes, with rolling hills to the south, and lofty mountains further away to the north. Unlike the farmer at

121

Polmont the innkeeper at Greenloaning did not try to over-charge us. " Anything you generally give " was his reply to my enquiry how much I was to pay. He seemed more than satisfied with two shillings.

We passed through Blackford and about 9 o'clock ate our frugal breakfast of coffee and cornflakes just beyond the entrance to the famous Gleneagles Hotel, where at the same moment a much more expensive and elaborate meal was doubtless being served to its guests.

Auchterarder, which was the next village we passed through, is one of the chief centres of the fruit picking. We noticed many fields of raspberries, on either side of the road.

A group of men and women who were tramping along on their way to berry picking passed us. One of the women was pushing two babies in a pram, four or five older bairns walked with the grown ups.

They hailed us and we stopped to talk with them. In summer time Perthshire is over-run with these often pathetic looking groups of fruit-pickers. Their wages are low, and in many cases the housing provided is scandalous. Sometimes they sleep in so-called dormitories—very often barns or even cowsheds. In spite of government regulations overcrowding is almost general.

Better off are the tinkers who live in their tents than the rest of the workers in their ' bothies,' ' chaumers ' and dormi-tories. On the other hand the summer fruit-picking in Scot-land is as much looked forward to in some of the tenements and closes of Edinburgh, Glasgow or Dundee, as the hop-picking in the slums of London. It ensures an annual ' country holiday ' for whole families and they return home in many instances all the better for the fresh air, and none the worse for the bad conditions in which they have been housed.

We stopped for lunch in a shady wood near Crossgates. The day was close and sultry, with several heavy showers of rain. Nothing exciting happened during what seemed to be a very long afternoon. At last Perth came into view, with a gradual descent into the suburbs. Then cobble streets and some painful jolting for the unfortunate driver.

While waiting for a few minutes outside a shop a little girl, in company with an elderly man, who seemed rather the worse for drink, came up to the van. Leaning on the shafts for support, he remarked, " My wee lassie would like to look inside." She herself said nothing, but from her expression it was clear that she was eager to climb up and have a peep into this fascinating ' wee hoosie' on four wheels. But shyness was stronger than curiosity, and she dared not venture.

The man began to talk in a maudlin manner, informing us that he himself could afford to buy a hundred or more cara-vans or any ' damn motor-car ' if he chose. " But give me horses," he said. " They're the best friends a man can have! " Then he staggered off, the little girl clutching his hand to prevent him from falling.

I found it difficult to realise that before the Reformation Perth was about the most Catholic town in Scotland, at least as regards the number of churches, chapels, and religious com-munities it contained within its boundaries. But little or no trace is left of the Carthusian, Dominican, and Franciscan monasteries—for after John Knox's famous sermon in 1559, they and the great parish church of St. John, with its forty altars, were ' purged of idolatry.'

For nearly three centuries Perth was without a resident priest, only being visited at rare intervals by itinerant mission-aries—the nearest Catholic chapel during the Penal Times being at Stobhall, about seven miles north of the burgh. One can picture these missionaries wandering about the country in disguise, their mass vestments and altar stone carried in a pack on their back. It is difficult to realise what hardships and privations they had to endure. It is recorded that one of them, the Rev. James McKay, would never risk taking his meals in a house, but used to make his porridge in some secluded spot out of sight of the road.

It was the Irish who brought back the Faith to Perth. By 1830 several hundred families had settled in the town and a small chapel was opened for their use, replaced in later years by the present Gothic church of St. John.

It was a stiff climb for the horses up Kinnoull Hill, from whose slopes the Redemptorist community looks down on the city of Perth, and far beyond to the mountains of the Central Highlands. The foundation of the church and monastery was due to the enthusiasm of Fr. Edward Douglas, C.SS.R., a member of the well known Scottish family of which the Marquis of Queensberry is the chief representative. As a convert to the Faith the re-Catholicising of his native land was always his chief preoccupation. The monastery was opened in 1869; the church, dedicated to Our Lady of Perpetual Succour, soon afterwards.

St. Mary's, Kinnoull, serves as the novitiate for the English province of the Redemptorists. One afternoon during our stay here, the novice master and his young men had a picnic tea outside the caravan and seemed to enjoy this unaccustomed change from the strict discipline of their normal life. Our supply of cups was not equal to the number of our guests, so we had to ask them to bring their own.

A story is told that Queen Victoria, on noticing this new group of buildings for the first time, asked what they were. Fearing to offend her Majesty's Protestant susceptibilities, her informer thought it more prudent to explain that they were " a sort of reformatory." In a sense this is true, but it would be more correct to describe Kinnoull as a Beacon of Catholicism in the very heart of Presbyterian Scotland.

TEN

Couper Angus—Glamis—a night with tinkers—Forfar—the old Irish tramp—Montrose—Stonehaven—Blairs College—Aberdeen.

We heard Mass at 6 o'clock, and got away from Kinnoull about an hour later. I walked with Bill behind the caravan as far as Scone. Here he was yoked, and we moved on at a good steady pace through pleasant country, mostly grassy fields broken up with woods. About midday we tethered the horses, who munched grass by the roadside while we had our own dinner. Six men stop and stare at the wagon for at least twenty minutes. As we move off I hail them with " Fine day," but they just continue to grin and stare and make no response.

At Coupar Angus I bought some groceries. Nothing much occurred during the afternoon. Tony pointed out to me various points of farming interest—the different ways of yoking the horses to that common in the north of England, remarking on the number of wire fences as compared with hedges, and the fine quality of the black cattle

We passed through Meigle, a straggling village of grey stone houses, many with red tiled roofs. There were big farms with tall chimneys like those which had so aroused my companion's curiosity in Berwickshire. A ' wee loonie ' was trudging home from school. We told him to jump up and we'd give him a lift. He accepted the invitation in a flash, but was far too shy to say much as he sat beside Tony.

" Look at those double-furrow rowing ploughs and three row scrufflers," he shouted to me while I was boiling the kettle for tea. I gave a glance in the direction indicated, but as the van was very shaky I felt it more prudent to concentrate on the movement of the Primus stove rather than study types of ploughs and scrufflers.

About 6 o'clock we drove into Glamis, a pretty little village with many trees. I asked the blacksmith where we could spend the night. He recommended the common, and told me to turn left until we were in sight of the railway.

We got a glimpse of the famous Castle. Noticing the flag flying from the tower we supposed Lord Strathmore must be in residence. "You ought to have called on him," said my companion. "He might have let the horses graze in his park. He's plenty of grass to spare." I was rather doubtful.

But we were entertained that night not by the Earl of Strathmore but by a party of tinkers whom we found had already taken possession of the common. They consisted of three families and three ponies; the latter being tethered on the grass to prevent them wandering away. I wondered how the ' tinks ' would receive us, but there was no cause for any alarm that our presence would be resented. The men greeted us in the most friendly manner, and helped Tony to unharness Jack and Bill, then found a good patch of ground where they could graze.

It was not long before they had satisfied their curiosity as to our business, and were only too ready to answer our questions as to their lives and customs. They told us that they spent the winter at Tain in Ross-shire. "We've got vans just like yours," one of the men said, "but when summer comes round we leave the vans and travel south with light carts and tents to Auchterarder. We work on the berry-picking. Then we sometimes move on a bit further, but we get back to Tain before the winter." Such was the uniform routine of the lives of these nomads.

While I was preparing supper two of these rough-looking men, dark haired and dark skinned, helped Tony to move one of the axle-blocks—the wheel which came off at Newcastle had never been quite right ever since. " Aye! That's a good job," remarked one of the men, watching Tony nailing on a horse-

shoe which had got loose. "I could na dee it better me
sel'." "So you do your own shoeing?" said Tony. "Aye!
I got twa new shoes on hind feet on Monday, and had to take
off and put on again th' nicht. Your artist-man ought to get
a tent like ours. Come and see it."

The tent, like the other two which were almost identical,
consisted of a light framework of bent wood, covered with
canvas, the inside stuffed up with rags, to keep out draughts.
It was about eight feet long, six feet wide, but no more than
four to five high even in the middle. So one had to stoop
when standing up inside—or squat on the ground. I offered
to take photos of the children, but was refused permission.
"It brings bad luck to us," was the explanation given. One
of the tinkers came from Lancashire and had the utmost contempt for everything Scottish. "They talk about the Devil's
Elbow, but it'd be nobbut a little bank in Lancashire. There
may be mountains in Scotland I grant, but there's no real
steep banks."

All the men were keen to swop horses with us—like almost
every gipsy or tinker we ever met in England or Scotland. It
certainly proved that Tony took good care of his two nags that
they should have aroused such covetousness in the breasts of
men who know more about horseflesh than any others. Finding that we had no intention of parting with either Jack or
Bill, they tried to tempt us to buy their harness—very 'decora-
tive' to look at with its silver plated ornaments, consisting of
no less than one hundred and fifty-six separate pieces. But
closer examination revealed the fact that the leather was rotten.

After supper I turned on the wireless and all the tinkers,
male and female, young and old, listened as if spellbound with
the music. They made a wonderful picture as they leaned
against the shafts of the van or sat on the steps. Dame Laura
Knight ought to have been there to paint it. Behind them
were their Arab-like tents, from which a faint coil of blue
smoke rose up against the orange glow of the sunset. They
listened and said very little—until at last I felt I had had

enough, so switched off the radio, and bade them good-night.

It would appear that the manner of life of the Scottish tinkers has not changed very much during the past hundred years, except for the abandoning of horses for internal combustion engines as a means of transport. Even as far back as about 1850, so Mr. Simson tells us in his *History of the Gipsies,* many of them were keeping shops for the sale of earthen-ware, china, and crystal. It was no unusual thing for more than £1,000 to be invested by a gipsy in his business. Many gipsies — ' Tinkers ' as they are usually called in Scotland—dealt in horses; some kept public-houses; others were coopers, shoemakers, plumbers, and masons. Not a few were itinerant bell-hangers, umbrella-makers, tinsmiths, braziers, and cutlers; while chimney sweeping was another common occupation. Mr. Simson tells us that these men were " scarcely to be distinguished as gipsies; yet they all retain the language, and converse in it among themselves." One is rather surprised to learn that quite a number of gipsy women became " ladies maids, and even housekeepers to clergymen and farmers." One had not realised that gipsies had invaded the Presbyterian manse, and Mr. Simson mentions more than one instance of a ' Scottish clergyman ' (admittedly a " dissenting " one) who had married a gipsy, although he admits that " in all probability he was not aware that he was taking a gipsy to his bosom; and as little did the public generally, but it was well known to the initiated that both her father and mother had cut and divided many a purse." Perhaps even more startling is the information that " the police establishments in large as well as small towns contain some of the fraternity." Mr. Simson explains this enabled gipsies to become the " instruments of affronting and punishing their hereditary enemies," and that " the lounging and idle kind of life, coupled with the activity of a constable, is pretty much to their natural disposition. An intelligent gipsy is calculated to make a first-rate constable and thief-catcher."

There were still several tribes of tinkers who retained the nomadic habits of their ancestors, just like those among whom we had camped at Glamis. The making of horn spoons was a profitable trade, as well as dealing in earthen-ware and tin. In certain parts of Scotland they became a serious nuisance, and as early as 1829 the *Caledonian Mercury* reported that " the country has been much infested of late by wandering hordes of vagabonds. The evil has increased rapidly of late, and calls loudly for redress. They generally travel in bands, varying in number from ten to thirty; and wherever they pitch their camps, the neighbours are certain of suffering loss of cattle or poultry, unless they submit to pay a species of blackmail to save themselves from heavier and more irregular contributions. These bands possess all the vices peculiar to the regular gipsies, without any of the extenuating qualities which distinguish those of foreign tribes. Unlike the latter they do not settle in one place sufficiently long to attach themselves to the soil, or to particular families; and seem possessed of no industrious habits, but those of plunder and knavery, and riot.." Perthshire was one of their favourite haunts, as well as Angus, but they often penetrated as far west as Argyll.

It would be hard to discover in these days a gipsy encampment anywhere in Scotland like that described by Mr. Simson at St. Boswells Fair about the middle of the last century. He tells us that " part of them formed their carts, laden with earthen-ware, into two lines, leaving a space between them, like a street. In the rear of the carts were a few small tents in which were gipsies, sleeping in the midst of the noise and bustle of the market; and numbers of children, horses, asses, and dogs, hanging around them. There were also kettles suspended from triangles in which victuals were cooking; and many of the gipsies enjoyed a warm meal, while others at the market had to content themselves with a cold repast. In the midst of this large and crowded fair, I noticed, without the least discomposure on their part, some of the male gipsies, changing their dirty, greasy-looking shirts for clean ones,

129

leaving no covering on their tawny persons, but their breeches; and some of the old females, with bare shoulders and breasts, combing their dark locks, like black horses tails, mixed with grey."

More akin to the friendly tinkers at Glamis was a band of tinsmiths which Mr. Simson came across in Fife, and which he thus describes: "The horde consisted of three married couples, the heads of as many families, one grown up, unmarried female, and six half-grown children below six years of age. Including the more grown-up members, scattered about in the neighbourhood, begging victuals, there must have been about twenty souls belonging to this band. The tinsmiths had two horses and one ass, for carrying their luggage, and several dogs. They remained, during three cold and frosty nights, encamped in the open fields, with no tents or covering for twenty individuals, but two pairs of old blankets. Some of the youngest children, however, were pretty comfortably lodged at night. The band had several boxes, or rather old chests, each about four feet long, two broad, and two deep, in which they carried their white-iron plates, working tools, and some of their infants, on the backs of their horses. In these chests the children passed the night, the lids being raised a little, to prevent suffocation. The stock of working tools, for each family, consisted of two or three files, as many hammers, a pair of bellows, a wooden mallet, a pair of pincers, a pair of large shears, a crucible, a soldering-iron or two, and a small anvil of a long shape, which was stuck into the ground."

We also read that the females as well as the males were employed in making tin utensils for household use, and that the clink of their hammers was heard from daybreak till dawn. Mr. Simson noted that "each family ate their meals by themselves, wrought at their calling by themselves, and sold their goods for themselves."

The costume of another itinerant band of tinkers he met with in Fife about 1855 is worthy of mention: "The party were very neatly attired, some the young girls having trousers with frills at their ankles." What Mr. Simson tells us about the iron constitutions of the tinkers still seems to be true, although I have never actually come across an instance of such spartan indifferance to cold, as the " no uncommon thing," he mentions of " a poor Scottish gipsy" wrapping himself and his wife in a thin torn blanket, and thus pass the night in the cold of December in the open air by the wayside. Perhaps the modern tinkers have grown more effeminate in their habits?

No matter where we came across tinkers or gipsies during our wanderings through England and Scotland, they always showed us the utmost kindness and politeness—in fact they were always ready to treat us as if we were actually one of themselves, and not merely ' amateur ' vagrants. They were always grateful for even the smallest effort to assist them, and I realised the truth of what I had often read—that a gipsy does not forget a service done to him. Two years after this caravan pilgrimage was over I happened to be staying in Sussex. One day when travelling in a motor bus across Ditchling Common, three extremely rough-looking, dark-skinned men boarded the bus and sat down behind me. A few moments later I was surprised to be hailed as if I were an old friend. The three men left their seats and shook hands with me and asked if I still had the caravan and horses; many other questions about my affairs, and what had become of my former companion. It was only after quarter of an hour or so that I remembered where we must have met them, and then I recalled that we had given them some butter or tea—I forget which. Anyhow they remembered me all right; and when we said good-bye on arriving at Brighton I was made to promise that if ever I wished to spend a few weeks on the roads again, there would always be a welcome in their vans or tents! They urged me to take up the life again, maintaining that it was the best sort of life for any man, but told me that of course I must have the right sort of wife to look after me, and that they could pro-vide a selection of suitable partners!

131

I received a very similar welcome not so long ago from some tinkers in Scotland, who seemed equally glad to meet me again. So I feel inclined to agree with Mr. Simson who tells us in his book that " the Scottish gipsies have ever been distinguished for their gratitude to those who treated them with civility and kindness, during their progress through the country," and my own experiences as well as that of my companion, prove conclusively that this often despised race is capable of giving one a lasting confidence, loyalty and friendship. Among the real gipsies the dignified courtesy of manner often reminded me of that of the Arabs I had conversed with in Palestine. One finds the same conventional methods of approach—the same verbal formulæ—the same vivid imagination and wealth of imagery in their conversation. It is no good being stand-offish or condescending, for the real gipsy believes—and quite rightly so—that he is one's equal; that it is blood which counts, not riches or external marks of worldly prosperity. One must treat him as a ' gentleman,' and he will treat one in the same manner. There was one particular gipsy whom I got to know in East Anglia, who never failed to call at my cottage whenever he was on his rounds collecting rags and bones, not that he ever did any business with me or got anything out of me, for he never begged. But when he discovered that I too had spent a year living in a caravan, like his own, and that I had met quite a number of his friends and relations during my travels, he ceased to treat me as a stranger; always addressing me by my Christian name. He would sit over a cup of coffee with the same dignity as an Arab chief, conversing with me in the same quiet liesurely manner of those whose homes are in the desert. Then after half an hour or so, he would get up and take his leave, promising to call again next time he was passing through the village on business. Incidentally he was a born artist, and I envied his skill in drawing horses—his efforts in this direction putting my own to shame. He could have taught me a lot if I had become his pupil. And once again I was invited most cordially to join the band to which he belonged and spend a month or two roaming East Anglia when the summer came round, for, as he assured me, there would be plenty to sketch, and he and his fellow vagrants would make me welcome as one of themselves. But more pressing engagements prevented me from accepting this invitation; however some day it may be possible to manage it.

When we got up next morning a heat mist shrouded the common. The tinkers and their families were still asleep; their tents firmly closed against fresh air or intruders. As there was nobody visible I took a photo of this encampment and hope I did not cast a spell on the sleepers by so doing. We got away without seeing any of the tinkers. It was still very early; not much more than 7 o'clock.

An hour or so later we reached Forfar where, on the outskirts of the town, we were surprised to meet another caravan almost the double of our own. It belonged to a ' dealer ' from Glasgow. Finding ourselves on a quiet road with hardly any traffic, and as we were in no great hurry, we decided to stop for an early lunch when we got to Montreathmont Moor. The horses grazed peacefully on the rich grass by the roadside.

About six miles before Montrose we came up to a tramp slowly plodding the road. " Shall we offer him a lift? " asked Tony. " Certainly," I answered. So Pat—as we called him— for the moment he opened his mouth the land of his origin was evident—clambered up on the van and settled himself into a corner beside the driver. I busied myself in getting tea ready, and overheard scraps of conversation . . . the Boer War . . . workhouse . . . France in 1914 . . . no work in Ireland . . . come to Scotland . . . not like the Old Country—hard folks . . . pick up jobs here and there. . . . ' Pat ' wasn't much to look at; his clothes ragged and worn —but he possessed the natural courtesy of the Celt, and gratefully accepted a cup of tea and some bread and butter, with profuse apologies for giving me so much trouble. His face lit up when he spotted the small crucifix hanging on the wall of the caravan, also a picture of Our Lady. Finding that he was among fellow Catholics, he gave vent to some not very complimentary opinions about Protestants. No! He didn't like Scotland or its religion.

We skirted the woods in which Rossie Castle used to stand until it was sold to a speculative builder for the sum of £1 (at least so I have been told) on condition that he would pull it down, I wondered what my great-grandfather, Horatio Ross, who built this sham fortress about a century ago, would have said if he had known what would be the fate of the mansion which must have cost him a small fortune.

On entering Montrose a friendly policeman advised me to try a small farm on Rossie Island where he thought there would be no trouble in finding grazing for the horses. He was right, and the farmer raised no objection to our spending the night in his field.

Hidden away in a side street I discovered St. Mary's Catholic Church, an unpretentious little Gothic structure, erected in 1886. There are not many resident Catholics in Montrose, which was one of the first places in Scotland to welcome Protestantism, largely owing to its intercourse with the Netherlands. It is unlikely that Mass was said here for over three centuries, so completely was the Old Religion uprooted.

We felt rather lazy the next morning and did not get away from Montrose until 9.30. Tony needed a new whip. I forget exactly how many he lost during our journeys! He managed to find just what suited him at a saddler's in the High Street. The saddler was much interested in the caravan.

" I'd like to see everyone with a turn-out like yours," he remarked approvingly. " It was a bad day for men like me when motor-cars came in. Now I have to try to make a living by selling sporting goods, and my shop window looks like a draper's, what with bathing costumes, cycling shorts, and so on."

Soon after entering Kincardineshire we caught up our Irishman of yesterday, still plodding along with his pack over his shoulder." I saw ye in town," he said, " but didn't want to bother ye." We told him to come aboard, and I stowed away his pack inside the van.

All that day we were in a thick sea-fog and at times could hardly make out the road twenty yards ahead of us. We passed the fishing village of Johnshaven, and stopped for dinner a mile beyond..

We had great difficulty in persuading Pat to share our meal. " I don't like to put on your good nature," was his way of excusing himself. " I'm like that, you see." He wouldn't eat much and when he had finished he slipped away over a stone dyke into a field. We did not see him again, and often wonder if he is still wandering round Scotland in the search for ' jobs ' of which he had heard rumours.

The fog turned to a drizzle during the afternoon. Tony and myself took spells in driving which made a change for both of us. Passing Dunottar Castle on the right, we descended the long ' brae ' into Stonehaven. Here, thanks to Fr. Murdoch, who was expecting our arrival, a good field for the horses had already been reserved at a farm just outside the town.

The farmer and Tony found it rather difficult to understand each other's respective dialects—but I think it was the former's Mearns variant of ' braid Scots ' which proved more baffling than the latter's ' Cleveland ' Yorkshire. I listened to them with amusement, and when they got completely mixed up came to their rescue as interpreter! I liked that farm—so typical of the Nor' East—just the sort of farm described with such precision and sure knowledge by the late J. Grassic Gibbon in his three novels—*Sunset Song, Cloud Howe,* and *Grey Granite.*

Kincardineshire has always remained a stronghold of Protestantism since the 16th century. None of the county families in the Mearns held on to the " Auld Kirk." Until the opening of the Gothic chapel of the Immaculate Conception in 1877,

St. Mary's, Stonehaven.

Stonehaven was served occasionally from Blairs College. " A chaste and elegant little structure " was the description given of the church by a contemporary journalist—personally I should call it ' toy-like,' for it bristles crockets and pinnacles and elaborate ornament. If the stone were white the effect would be not unlike a wedding cake.

Fr. Murdoch invited the two of us to breakfast with him after Mass. About 11 o'clock we left Stonehaven, climbed up a long brae and found ourselves in bleak country of heather moors, peat bogs, pine woods, and stone dykes. For senti-mental reasons I asked Tony to stop outside Netherley House on the excuse that I wanted a cup of coffee! But it was really because about seventy years ago my great-grandfather, Horatio Ross, at that time M.P. for Aberdeen, had been Laird of Netherley, and my mother lived here as a small baby. I felt I wanted to fix in my memory the character and look of the place and its surroundings.

So we moved on and descended from this high land into the valley of the Dee, where a glorious view of mountains con-fronted us. It was Saturday afternoon and the main road was thronged with motorists and cyclists rushing out from Aber-deen on their way to Ballater, Braemar, or Aboyne. Lads in shorts, lassies in trousers—all turn round and have a good stare at our caravan and horses. So too do a crowd of chil-dren, a Sunday School no doubt, who were enjoying themselves under the trees at Mill Inn.

We passed the front of Blairs College and turned up a drive at the far side which led to the farm buildings. But here we had to turn back again and go a long way round the way we had already come, for the van was about an inch too high to get under an archway. The road—if it deserves to be called a road—was about the bumpiest we had ever met with. How-ever we were given a friendly welcome by the rector, Mgr. Cronin, and the college grieve, who directed Tony where to ' park ' the van, and after the horses had been unharnessed, led them away to a distant field where they had a good rest and feed during the week-end we spent at Blairs.

I am writing up my diary sitting on the steps on the wagon in this quiet corner behind the farm, above which rise up the roofs and towers and spire of the vast group of granite buildings which make up St. Mary's College.

The silver grey granite walls of Blairs College stand out in vivid contrast to the green woodlands which surround them, especially when viewed from the north side of the Dee. For more than a century Blairs has been the ' nursery ' for the Catholic priests of Scotland. It was founded in 1829, the property having been handed over to the Vicars Apostolic by Menzies of Pitfodels. The first students were brought here from the seminary at Aquhorties, near Inverurie, founded in 1800, to replace the older seminary at Scalan, Glenlivet. Other students came from the college on the Isle of Lismore, near Oban. For over sixty years the Pitfodels mansion housed successive generations of students for the Scottish priesthood. But it had become far too small and cramped for modern requirements. In 1892, the then rector, Fr. Aeneas Chisholm, afterwards Bishop of Aberdeen, decided to rebuild the college on a much more ambitious scale. To his wide vision and undaunted enthusiasm are due the modern buildings of Blairs, the first part of which was opened in October, 1898.

There is much to be seen at Blairs College; its famous library contains all that remains of the ancient library of the Scots College in Paris, and many other valuable treasures. Here we gazed with interest at the portrait of Mary Queen of Scots, found hidden away at Douai, after the French Revolution.

This morning it was a rare treat to listen to the Plain Chant Mass, perfectly rendered by the choir of boys. If only the setting had been as beautiful as the music! But I must confess that I always feel that this ornately decorated college chapel is one of the most unsatisfactory examples of modern ecclesiastical architecture in Scotland. Still one can always shut one's eyes and not one's ears!

To-day being the Sunday within the Octave of Corpus Christi we were able to take part in the open-air procession of the Blessed Sacrament through the college grounds, when the singing of the boys was something which I shall not forget in a hurry. I have assisted at many Corpus Christi processions during the quarter of a century I have been a Catholic, and the one at Blairs made a special impression on me.

Tony and I went into Aberdeen one morning to do some shopping, and I took the opportunity to make a sketch of the interior of St. Peter's, Justice Street. It would be difficult to describe this church as beautiful, but it is a lovable little place, with a devotional atmosphere not often found in Scotland, where the practice of making visits to the Blessed Sacrament has never become common, except in the industrial districts of the south where the Irish element preponderates.

St. Peter's is approached through a close, and quite hidden from the street, no doubt for reasons of security. Here the famous ' Priest Gordon ' carried on his devoted apostolate among the poor during the 18th and early years of the 19th centuries. The foundation-stone of the chapel was laid on April 15th, 1803, and opened by Bishop Cameron in August the following year. In my drawing you will notice the shrine of Our Lady of Aberdeen. The statue is a replica of the image once venerated in Aberdeen Cathedral. It was taken to Belgium after the Reformation and after wandering about has found a home in the Church of Notre Dame de Finistère at Brussels. Efforts have been made to induce the owners to return the image to Scotland, but so far without success. However the shrine in St. Peter's, Justice Street, is seldom without worshippers. It is not often that you visit the church and do not find many votive candles burning before Our Lady of Aberdeen.

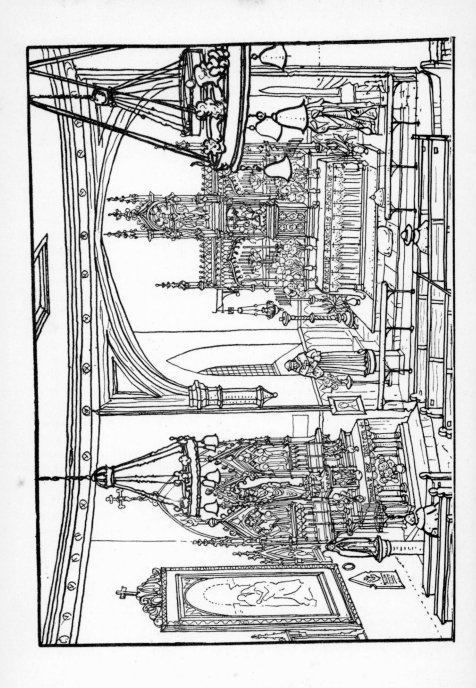

St. Peter's, Aberdeen.

ELEVEN

Getting away from Blairs proved almost as difficult as arriving. For Jack jumped a fence and had to be chased all round a field by Tony and the grieve before he was caught. They led him back to the farm, where after a drink of water he submitted to being harnessed. Once more we bumped along that rough cart-track and were glad to reach the main road. This we followed as far as Mill Inn. Here we turned right and crossed the Dee. Bill never liked bridges and it took some persuasion before he would venture on to this one.

We stopped at Mary Culter to do some shopping. "You've a hilly road before you get to Huntly," an old man informed Tony. "Aye! But it's a gran' life. An' what a bonnie pair of horses."

Leaving Mary Culter we turned right, passing through bleak treeless country, where as Tony remarked it looks as if a giant had been playing about with granite boulders, and then run away and left them.

We stopped for a few minutes outside the lodge gates of Dunecht, one of the many ostentatious erections put up by the late Lord Cowdray who seemed determined to ' leave his mark ' on Aberdeenshire. The stone dykes which surround his vast estates are another striking feature. They seem to express the whole mentality of this millionaire Yorkshire contractor.

From Dunecht one road led past Castle Fraser, one of the finest examples of ' Scottish Baronial ' architecture, a glimpse of which could be obtained through the dense woods which surround it on almost every side.

141

Benachie—that famous Aberdeenshire mountain—now appeared on our left as we dropped down into the valley of the Don. We crossed the river at Kemnay, a straggling village of no great interest.

I was uncertain exactly where the Catholic church at Fetternear was located, but as we were moving along a quiet country lane, we sighted its roof hidden among trees to our right. On reaching the drive which led up to it I wondered if the caravan would be able to pass, for the boughs of the trees so badly needed clipping that there was scarcely room to get beneath them. Our chimney barely escaped being knocked off.

Fr. Colin Macdonald allowed us to leave the caravan in front of the church, but came with us to a neighbouring crofter who let us put the horses in one of his fields. It seemed that he was a regular reader of the *Universe* and said to Tony, who had remarked on the quality of the grass in the meadow, " Why, no grass could be too good for the Pilgrim Artist's horses." I hope Jack and Bill realise how privileged they are on account of their master!

The lands of Fetternear belonged to the Bishops of Aberdeen in pre-Reformation times. They were conveyed to the family of William Leslie of Balquhain in 1566 by the last Catholic Bishop of Aberdeen, William Gordon. Leslie had protected the Cathedral from destruction by a mob in 1560. The grant was confirmed by Pope Clement X in 1670, and renewed by Pius IX in 1870. These historic events are recorded in the stained glass windows of the present church, a well proportioned grey granite building opened in 1869.

The mansion of Fetternear was burnt down some years ago, and as I wandered round its now overgrown ruins on that June evening, I recalled the tragic history of the great family of Leslie who at one time were so powerful in Aberdeenshire that, even in the times of most bitter persecution, they generaally managed to keep a priest in their households. In 1714 the local Presbyterian minister complained with indignation of the

Our Lady of the Garioch and St. John, Fetternear.

chapel at Fetternear, "put to no use but idolatrous worship." To-day it is only the birds who chant the praise of their Creator within the charred ruins of Fetternear.

I left the ruins and wandered on to the Old Kirk of St. Ninian, now disused, which stands beside the river Don. Here Bishop Hay was laid to rest in 1811. He died at the neighbouring seminary of Aquhorties, to which I made my way after leaving the church. The buildings still remain in much the same state as when they housed the lads who were being educated for the Scottish priesthood, and among whom Bishop Hay passed his last years.

We left Fetternear about 9.30 after Mass and breakfast, and took a short cut. "It's rough country as well as a rough road," said Tony as he looked at the stony fields and the jagged outline of Benachie which rose up on our left. Having jogged along for about five miles we stopped to give the horses a feed while we ourselves had a cup of coffee.

A few miles further we stopped again beside the famous Maiden Stone, and examined the curious carvings with which its sides are covered. We wondered what could be the meaning of the dog, elephant, comb and mirror. An elephant in Aberdeenshire seems rather exotic.

There was a long pull up over the Foudland Hills; bleak exposed country, once the dread of travellers in winter when the road was often blocked with snow drifts. There were fine views over rolling farm lands as we descended into Huntly which we reached about 7 o'clock.

I called at the presbytery where Mgr. Mulligan told me he had arranged for us to park the caravan in a field near the ruins of the castle. A place of many memories, for it was long the home of the Earls of Huntly, once the most powerful family in this part of Scotland. They remained Catholic for more than a century after the Reformation, and generally managed to keep a priest as chaplain.

Our camp site was picturesque, but we wished the midges had been less ravenous. But they were nothing to what we had to endure later on in the West Highlands.

While we were eating our supper a policeman came to have a look at us and find out what was our business. However I managed to convince him we were quite harmless even if we did look like tinkers.

Remembering the drastic treatment meted out to gipsies and " peer fowk " in Aberdeenshire during the 17th and 18th centuries I was relieved to find this Huntly policeman did not order us to leave the town at once, or even send us back to England as did the Aberdeen baillies when dealing with vagrants. In spite of their efforts they were not always successful for in the *Old Statistical Account* we are told that the parish of Peterculter was " often infested with vagrants of various descriptions, who by threats or otherwise, compel people to give them money and the best *vivres* their houses afford. They likewise pick up poultry, apparel, and what they can lay hold of. Their exactions are oppressive, their numbers often formidable, and it hurts the feelings of the humane to see so many young people trained up to the same pernicious courses."

Andrew Fletcher of Saltoun, writing about 1698 informs us in the *Second Discourse on the Affairs of Scotland,* that there were " about one hundred thousand of those vagabonds who had lived without any regard or subjection either to the laws of the land or even those of God and Nature." He gives a grim picture of how " they meet together in the mountains, where they feast and riot for many days; and at country weddings, markets, burials, and the like public occasions, they are to be seen—both men and women—perpetually drunk, cursing, blaspheming, and fighting together." I hope the Huntly policeman did not take us for one of this crowd of vagabonds. If so he might have recommended (like his famous 17th century countryman) to have us "presented to the government of the state of Venice to serve in the gallies against the common enemy of Christendom, under pain of scourging." In 1700 a gipsy named James McPherson was condemned to death at Banff on a charge of ' thieving, purse-cutting, and other crimes

145

of masterful bangstrie and oppression.'

But not all the 18th century vagrants were gipsies, some were Irish who came to Scotland " on the pretence of visiting their relatives." There were likewise a vast crowd of beggars of Scottish origin, greatly despised and hated by the genuine gipsies, and who shared none of the better qualities of the latter.

I went to Mass the following morning, and found myself in a curious octagonal shaped building unlike any church I have ever seen. I remember having read an account of its opening in the *Catholic Directory* for 1834, where it is described as a " new and splendid chapel." The writer went on to tell how funds for its erection were provided by Mr. John Gordon, of the family of Wardhouse, then living at Cadiz. There can be little doubt that his association with Spain must have influenced the style of architecture. Incidentally it was the first Catholic chapel in Scotland to be provided with a bell since the Reformation. What a sensation it must have caused when that bell rang out for the first Mass when, so we are told, the choir of St. Peter's, Aberdeen, " executed several pieces of sacred music in a very superior style." No doubt it scandalised some of the older worshippers who would not have forgotten Bishop Hay's strict injunctions against any kind of singing at Mass, as being a dangerous novelty.

I found breakfast ready for me on my return from Mass. Tony always protested he was no cook, but this was really false modesty. The midges were no better that morning. They found the unprotected flanks of Jack and Bill provided a satisfying meal, and Tony decided to rub them down with parafin. The smell certainly seemed to be effective.

After doing some shopping we got away about 11.30. This was the hottest day we had so far met with, and both of us cast off as many clothes as we could, finding a shirt and trousers quite sufficient.

Crossing the Deveron we left Aberdeenshire and entered

SANCTE MARGARITE
1834

P.F.ANSON.

9:6:1934.

St. Margaret's, Huntly.

Banffshire. Following the wooded bank of the river we soon reached the village of Rothiemay. I had received an invitation from Colonel Ian Forbes of Rothiemay Castle to call here, but when the caravan passed under the battlemented archway leading into the drive (the chimney only just clearing), the lodgekeeper came rushing out in a state of wild excitement.

" You cannot go up there," she exclaimed in horrified tones. " The Colonel doesn't allow tinkers in his grounds, and this drive only leads to the Castle. You must turn round at once."

I smiled at her, and she looked completely mystified when I explained that the Colonel was expecting me to lunch with him and that it was already after one o'clock. She realised that we couldn't be ordinary tinkers, but what on earth should the Deputy Lieutenant of Banffshire mean by inviting such strange guests to his table was too much for her powers of imagination.

Gazing at the caravan and me, and not knowing what to do, she said. "Well it's not my fault if the Colonel objects. I've done my best to stop you."

Tony drove on up the long avenue with rhododendrons in full bloom on either side. Just as we got to the stables a martial looking figure in a kilt appeared round a corner. Tony, who had never before seen a Scottish laird on his native heath got rather a shock. But any nervousness he may have felt, was at once dispelled when the laird started to help him to unharness the horses, in the manner of an expert.

After luncheon the Colonel showed us round the Castle, typical of many another in Scotland with its immensely thick walls, crow step gables and queer little turrets. We were taken to the recently excavated ruins of the old church, built on the site of a chapel founded in the 6th century by St. Drostan, a disciple of St. Columba. We gazed at the even more ancient stone circle, a Scottish Stonehenge, with its altar marked with stars, only clearly visible on Midsummer Eve.

I could write much more of Rothiemay Castle; its little

chapel where Mass is said from time to time; its many historic portraits and other treasures collected in the course of centuries.

It is good to feel that this famous old Scottish home has now come back into Catholic hands, and three of the present generation of Forbes have found religious vocations—the eldest son, formerly an officer in the Grenadier Guards, being a Benedictine monk at Ampleforth, and two of his sisters Canonesses Regular of the Lateran.

It was not until nearly six that we managed to get away from our host. Three hours later we come in sight of Portsoy. It was still broad daylight when we sat down to supper about 11 o'clock, for Tony had to take the horses to a farm some distance away. We received a most friendly welcome from the parish priest, Fr. James Bonnyman—indeed was there any place in Scotland where the priests did not welcome us and put themselves to no end of bother in making provision for man and beast? The caravan was parked beside the " chapel," as the Catholic church is invariably called in Scotland; the word " Kirk " being confined to Presbyterian places of worship. Even more tired than usual after this long day and the heat, we fell asleep about midnight.

The Catholic Church at Portsoy, dedicated to Our Lady of the Annunciation, was built by the Rev. Alexander Grant just over a century ago. It is typical of many others erected in the north-east of Scotland at that period; plain solid little churches, with no fuss or nonsense about them. They are a material expression, so one might say, of that sturdy deep-rooted faith which had managed to survive three hundred years of persecution. A type of Catholicism that lends literary expression in the writings of Bishop Hay; a kind of piety which is litterally foreign to the rush and hurry of present day life.

When the church was built the congregation numbered about five hundred. The priest also served Banff and Aberchirder. To-day the Catholics in and around Portsoy have

Church of the Annunciation, Portsoy.

decreased to no more than seventy. Most of them live too far away to get to Mass regularly, and the normal Sunday morning congregation seldom exceeds twenty. The lonely life of a priest in such a place as this cannot be easy, and it demands a peculiar vocation to carry on year after year.

We spent an enjoyable Sunday at Portsoy, a small fishing village which I have known and loved for nearly twenty years. It became quite famous in 1936 as the home port of the drifter "Boy Andrew" which won the Madame Prunier trophy for the biggest shot of herring during the East Anglican Autumn season. It seemed strange that it should need the enterprising proprietoress of a fashionable London restaurant to bring Portsoy into the newspaper headlines!

Tony had to go into Banff the following morning to visit a saddler, a new strap being needed for the harness. So it was not until well on in the afternoon that we drove away from Portsoy. I knew the road very well indeed and as we passed by the fishing villages of Sandend, Cullen and Portknockie, recalled many days in byegone years when I had sketched their harbours and little grey houses. To-day with a bright sun, blue sky and sea, they looked as attractive as ever.

About a mile before reaching Buckie I was pleased to find my old friend "Jeems" Clark, a fisherman with whom I had spent some happy times at sea in his father's drifter, on the look out for us. He greeted us warmly and said he had been waiting nearly on hour. I apologised and explained that we had been later in leaving Portsoy than I had intended. "Jeems" climbed up into the caravan and remarked that it rolled almost as much as a fishing boat.

"You don't feel sea sick, do you?" I asked.

Jack and Bill had grazed in many strange fields during their long journey, but it was a new experience for them to find themselves in sole possesion of the football ground of the "Buckie Thistles."

We failed to get in with the caravan for the entrance gate

was far too low. So in the end it rested on a plot of grass land in Duguid Street. Here live the McWilliam family who, as on many previous occasions, gave me the expected welcome. It was not long before my companion had made himself equally at home in their midst.

Tony found much to interest him at the harbour. I introduced him to some of my fishermen friends who initiated him into the mysteries of their craft. He became so fascinated that I began to wonder if he would be abandoning his horses and taking to the sea for a change. In fact he did talk seriously of going out for a night's fishing in the Moray Firth, but eventually decided it was better not to do so in case he could not get back on the day we had arranged to leave Buckie.

When I first got to know the Moray Firth coast nearly twenty years ago all the fishing villages were in an extremely prosperous condition. The fishermen were in possession of smart and well cared for steam drifters, and many of them lived in houses which they had built for themselves regardless of expense. They were a proud, independent community. But a few years after the war the herring industry began to decline, and a series of unremunerative seasons culminated in 1934 when hundreds of families found themselves reduced to absolute poverty. The average Scotsman, still less the average Englishman, knew or cared much how or where his breakfast herring was caught. He did not realise that fresh herrings were only a very small part of the industry on which over 80,000 of his fellow countrymen depended for a living before the War.

The far reaching international complications involved in the closing of " foreign markets " for cured herring were of little interest to the general public until comparatively recently.

Buckie, and most of the other ports on the Moray Firth Coast are sad places to-day. Few of the young lads feel any wish to become fishermen and find it more profitable in the long run to stop at home and live on the dole—or the

St. Peter's, Buckie.

" buroo " as they call it. These once prosperous towns and villages have acquired almost the same atmosphere of hopeless despair that one finds in the depressed areas of South Wales or Co. Durham. What is to be their future time alone can show.

There are certain persons who seem to feel that the Scottish herring industry will pass into the hands of English companies and vessels owned and financed from England. This would be sad fate for what was formerly one of the most profitable industries in Scotland. Is it too late to avert such a national disaster?

Buckie has a large Catholic population, being situated in the Enzie district, always one of the strongholds of the old Religion throughout the Penal Times. Until 1832 the nearest place of worship was at Preshome, about three miles distant, where the Vicar's Apostolic usually resided. In that year a temporary chapel was opened; replaced by the present building in 1857. A contemporary journalist described it as " altogether a most splendid church," but the Presbyterian fishermen looked upon it with horror and alarm. The twin spires, visible many miles out at sea, were referred to as " Yon twa horns o' the Deil." Catholics often called it the " cathedral."

The interior was enlarged and redecorated by the late Mgr. Provost Mackintosh, a much loved priest who spent many years in Buckie. He was immensely proud of the extremely ornate marble High Altar and reredos, designed by Charles Ménart, and I often found it difficult to hide my own feelings when he was praising its beauty to me.

One day during this stay in Buckie I made a sketch of St. Ninian's, Tynet; having heard rumours that the oldest Post-Reformation Catholic Church in Scotland was in danger of being replaced by a modern structure. When the Rev. Alexander Godsman built this low long barn like structure in 1755 he took the precaution of turning sheep into it lest its ultimate purpose should be discovered. It would not have been safe to have advertised of a Popish Mass House at that date.

Even to-day when passing along the main road from Cullen to Fochabers you would never suspect that the building is a Catholic church. It was enlarged in 1787 when the congregation was much more numerous than to-day. Dry-rot is spreading and the roof has been shored up to prevent collapse. The walls too are likely to give way. It is a pity this historic sanctuary cannot be scheduled as a National Monument. But few pilgrims seem to visit this " Banffshire Bethlehem " as it well deserves to be called. The interior, with its delightfully " primitive " Gothic altar is unique. There is an old pulpit and surrounding board; also a gilt door suspended above the altar, said to have been brought here from the chapel which formerly stood in St. Ninian's cemetary, a mile or so beyond Tynet. Here are buried Bishop Nicolson, the first Vicar Apostolic in Scotland, and many other missionary priests.

That same afternoon I also revisited St. Gregory's, Preshome. This most interesting church dates from 1788 and was the first attempt after the Reformation to build a Catholic place of worship to *look like a church.* Over the door is a tablet bearing the curious inscription " DEO 1788." As many visitors have remarked it is not often that you find a church dedicated to Almighty God in this uncompromising manner.

The West front remains unspoilt, except that one or two of the Grecian urns on the parapet have fallen down. A Gothic Sanctuary and an elaborately carved reredos, designed by Peter Paul Pugin, have completely altered the effect of the interior.

TWELVE

Keith—Dufftown—Glenlivet—Tombae—Scalan—Forres
—Elgin—Inverness—Eskadale.

The weather broke the morning we left Buckie and it seemed quite strange to be driving with rain on our faces. Our departure had not been without certain thrills. Having led down Jack and Bill from the football ground where they had become very fresh after four days' peaceful rest, we tethered the latter to some iron railings in front of our hosts' garden while we were harnessing Jack. He got excited and pulled off a large piece of the iron-work! Apologising for the damage we drove away, amid much waving and cheers from our kind friends and their relations.

Passing through the hamlet of Clochan, we climbed up the long hill to the summit of Aultmore. The rain ceased within a mile or so of Keith, and for the rest of the afternoon the sun was too hot to be pleasant.

No more striking proof of the survival of Catholicism in the north-east of Scotland during the Penal Times could be found than the large number of churches erected in Banff-shire within the first ten years after Catholic Emancipation. One of the most striking of these churches is St. Thomas', Keith, an imposing building in the Doric style, which was opened in 1831. The façade is said to be a ' free adaptation ' of S. Maria degli Angeli at Rome. The altar piece was presented by King Charles X of France, at that time living in exile at Holyrood Palace. As you will see from my sketch the church has a somewhat foreign-looking appearance, yet it does not seem out of place among the wide streets of grey stone houses which surround it. The copper dome is a recent addition to the church, which was enlarged from the designs of Charles Ménart.

St. Thomas', Keith.

We left Keith behind us and made our way through the valley of the Isla. We passed two small boys on the road who stopped to stare at us. Summoning up his courage one of them asked if this was the Pilgrim Artist's caravan. He told us that he had been following our journey every week in the *Universe* and seemed very proud to meet us.

We had tea near Drummuir, where the road winds along above a narrow gorge, with dense woods on either side. About six o'clock we drove into Dufftown, a quiet little town with whisky distilleries and cloth mills. Here we managed to find a good field behind the Catholic church with plenty of space in which the horses could roam about.

I have a great affection for the little church of Our Lady of the Assumption at Dufftown. This is one of the oldest missions in the north-east of Scotland. Even during the worst persecutions of the 17th and 18th centuries a priest was generally found in this part of Banffshire. Living in constant danger of being arrested, imprisoned and banished, these heroic missionaries ministered to their scattered flock in the parishes of Mortlach, Aberlour, and the Cabrach.

For a while they had no permanent centre. But during the 18th century chapels—if they deserve the name—were built at Shenval and Keithock. In spite of its secluded position the latter chapel was discovered by the English soldiers, who set fire to it after the Battle of Culloden. Mass was then said in private houses, or in lofts over farm buildings, at Tullochallum and elsewhere. The chapel at Keithock dates from about 1790, and is really no more than a bare loft above the cottage which served as a presbytery.

In 1817 the modern village of Dufftown was laid out. The Rev. John Gordon, then stationed at Keithock, obtained land from the Earl of Fife upon which he erected the present church which was opened in July, 1825. From the point of view of architecture it is of the greatest interest. To have built a Gothic vaulted roof at that period was indeed the last word of ' modernism.' Mr. John Gordon must have been a priest of wide culture, for he has left another proof of his efforts to promote a more dignified standard of worship than which was common at that date in the shape of a book of Church Music, which contains both Masses, motets and hymns. It was the first publication of its kind to be issued in Scotland since the Reformation and it continued to be used in many places until quite recently.

I must confess that I regret the removal of that curious domed shaped baldachino (reminiscent of the Brighton Pavilion) which surmounted the High Altar. It had been put up by the Rev. John Kemp in 1858 and I cannot recall any other example quite like it. Mr. John Devlin's new marble altar and oak reredos are more liturgically ' correct ' but they lack the charm and originality of the old baldachino, which was discovered to be so badly affected with dry rot that it had to be destroyed.

I think that Tony will chiefly remember Dufftown as the place where it was so hot. It surprised him to find that there could be really hot weather in the far north of Scotland. While I was sketching the interior of the church my companion took Bill to be shod. Jack rushed round the field as he always did whenever he was separated from his mate. It was amusing to watch the welcome which took place when Bill returned from the blacksmith's.

We got away about 3.30 in the afternoon, having decided that it was too hot to make an earlier start. Our road lay up Glen Rinnes and we had a long climb to over 1,000 feet above sea level. We stopped for tea near a drinking trough which had been erected in commemoration of the Coronation of King Edward VII. We were grateful to the donor, whoever he was; for not only the horses but also their drivers enjoyed a drink of the ice cold water on that sweltering afternoon.

The country became wilder; farm lands giving place to small crofts, and then moor and bog. Down into Glenlivet, past a comfortable looking manse where the minister and his wife were sitting beneath the shade of a tree on the lawn. They stopped talking and stared hard at the caravan. Tony waved to them; the lady gave him a gracious smile but the minister didn't respond to the salutation of ' tinkers.'

The road twisted and turned as it followed the course of the river. I pointed out the famous Minmore distillery to my companion, and then, on reaching the hamlet of Tomnavoulin, we turned left along a narrow road. I walked on ahead as I wanted to find out from the priest, who was awaiting our arrival, where the horses were to graze. It was about nine o'clock when we arrived at Tombae, which merely consists of a Catholic church, presbytery, school and cemetery. No other houses are visible but there are many small crofts hidden away in the surrounding hills. Fr. Bennett had almost given up hope of our arrival that night. He pointed out a field for the horses and told us that we could park the van in a yard behind the ' chapel house.'

It was so hot that we decided to sleep in our little tent in preference to the stuffy caravan which felt like an oven. But we were rudely awakened about 4 a.m. It was raining hard and the water had found its way through the canvas. I roused my companion and we made a hasty retreat into the caravan; one of us laden with blankets, the other with pillows. Then the rain ceased. But we were not going to risk another wetting so spent the rest of the night in the van. There was no need to rise early that Sunday morning for at Tombae, as in most of the country missions in the Aberdeen diocese, there is only one Mass and that at 11 o'clock, except once a month when there is an ' Early Service ' (to borrow an expression which I remember in my Anglican childhood). On informing a zealous young priest in the south of England of this custom he remarked, " They must be quite ' Low Church ' up there. Do they go in for Evening Communion as well? " But the explanation may be found in the conservative habits of the older people who have the same feelings about the reception of the Sacraments as did their grandparents, and who seldom went to Holy Communion more than four or five times a year. Old traditions are clung to tenaceously and are not easily uprooted in the country missions in the North East. At the same time it must be remembered that the majority of the congregations live some distance from the ' chapels.' It is not easy for farmers or crofters to get to an early Mass without serious inconvenience.

Glenlivet has always remained one of the most Catholic districts in Scotland. Around the hamlet of Tomnavoulin where the church is situated, there has always been a more or less regular succession of priests since Mr Francis Carolan, who was stationed here between 1687 and 1701. I was delighted with the church at Tombae, a Gothic structure erected in the year of Catholic Emancipation. In a contemporary description of the opening function much praise is given to the " elegant Gothic front of fine polished granite." The same writer informs us that the priest " will gladly accommodate two or three respectable Catholics as boarders," and suggests that " to persons of retired and religious habits, the situation will be most eligible, the climate most salubrious, and the scenery altogether beautiful and picturesque." I wonder if any ' respectable Catholics of retired and religious habits ' took advantage of the invitation and came to live as paying guests in the ' chapel house '?

Tombae certainly seemed a charming spot during the three days we spent there and nothing could have exceeded the kind hospitality shown us by Fr. Bennett behind whose presbytery the caravan rested.

One afternoon I set out across the moors to walk to the Braes of Glenlivet, a remote district cut off from the outside world and shut in on every side by mountains. In about three miles I reached the hamlet of Chapeltown where in 1827 a little church was built by the Abbé Paul Macpherson, who as a contemporary writer informs us, also provided " a small but comfortable dwelling house and appendages for the clergyman, as well as all the necessary vestments and furniture." In 1908

PFANSON. 18·6. 1924.

Tombae, Glenlivet.

the old chapel was replaced by a beautiful church designed by Archibald Macpherson. Few modern Catholic churches in Scotland seem so perfectly in harmony with their surroundings as this building with its rough harled walls and simple round-headed windows.

The ornate richness of the interior was a surprise to me. But how entirely satisfactory is the clever mingling of vivid scarlet, green and gold on the walls and ceiling. If only church architects would take a hint from those of Scandinavia and realise how much better their interiors would be for white walls as a foil to bright colour decoration!

From Chapeltown I took a rough track through fields and then across rough moorland. My way led me still further into the heart of the Braes where the steep mountains seemed to prevent any further advance. Had I not been told I should not have suspected that I should eventually come to a farm house, for it lay hidden behind a low ridge. This humble building was used as a seminary during the 18th century. Within its walls were educated more than a hundred priests between 1717 and 1799.

It must have been a thrilling experience to have been present in the little chapel of Scalan on that morning in 1725 when Bishop Gordon ordained two students to the priesthood. An even more memorable event was the episcopal consecration of George Hay in 1769. This saintly bishop often resided in the college and loved to share in the austere life and simple pleasures of the young students. After the battle of Culloden Scalan was burnt down by English soldiers, but was rebuilt a few years later. In 1799 the college was abandoned and the students removed to Aquhorties, which, as I have already related, we had visited during our stay at Fetternear.

It was sad to find this venerable sanctuary in such a neglected state. For over a century it has been used as a farm, and its present condition is a reproach to its owners. It is a pity that Scalan cannot be purchased by the Scottish bishops and put to a better use. For it is witness to the fidelity and loyalty of Scottish Catholics during the worst times of persecution. Moreover Scalan recalls to those outside the Fold of Peter that Catholicism in modern Scotland is not an alien religion imported from Ireland as many of them would have one believe. I made two sketches of the buildings and it was nearly dusk by the time I got back to Tombae.

The following afternoon Tony and I went to Tomintoul by motor bus as I wanted to make a sketch of the church in this very Catholic village, situated on a windswept plateau, 1,160 feet above the sea.

On our return to Tombae Fr. Bennett invited us to supper. Tony will always remember his first taste of real Glenlivet whisky. He sipped it with relish and soon became somewhat loquacious. However he may protest that his companion was more argumentative than usual. Anyhow neither of us had to put the other to bed.

We set the alarm clock at 5.30 for we had a long journey ahead of us and an early start was essential if we were to reach Forres that same day. Jack was unusually tiresome that morning, and in the end Bill had to be put into the shafts to pull the van out of the yard on to the road.

A thin drizzling rain damped our spirits and did not help to improve our tempers. However by the time we had reached Ballindalloch and crossed the Spey at Blacksboat, the rain had ceased and the sun came out. As we were jogging along two carts passed us and we were surprised to notice that in each instance the horses shied at the caravan. This was the first time such a thing had ever happened. And if I remember rightly it was on this morning that Jack and Bill first showed signs of their dislike of tar barrels. What exactly was the reason of this peculiar fear of anything in the shape of a barrel always remained a mystery. Anyhow we soon learned to be cautious whenever we saw barrels ahead of us, and to keep a good hold on the reins.

We now entered Morayshire. Tony was always proud when

he could add a new county to his list which by this time numbered about thirty.   It made him feel more and more of a
hardened traveller.

Our road climbed up over wide moorlands, the views in
every direction become more extensive as we proceeded. The
surface might have been better for only the wheel tracks had
tar-mac on them. We reached the summit about 2 p.m. Here
we had a late luncheon, letting the horses graze among the
scrubby grass and heather. We were now well over 1,000
feet up and the air was quite cold, so we preferred to shelter
within the van rather than picnic outside.

We had been warned that the road over the moors had a bad
surface, but so far it had been tolerable. But within quarter
of a mile from where we had stopped for lunch we realised
only too well that the warnings were correct, for never in all
our journeys did we again meet such an appalling surface. It
would be better to describe it as loose shingle and stones. We
began to fear serious damage to the van would be the penalty
for not having listened to good advice. After a mile or two
of terrific bumps and jolts I noticed that one of the brass axle
caps was missing. I walked back some distance but could not
find it. So we went on again, and were thankful to reach
the village of Dallas where we found ourselves on ordinary
roads again. We passed a tinkers' camp. Two of the men
accosted me and made envious remarks about our 'bonny pair
of horses.' Well might they do so, for their own nags were
skinny looking beasts.

It was getting late when we drove into Forres. People stared
at the caravan, evidently thinking we were part of a circus, and
disappointed not to see elephants or camels in our wake. Fr.
Lewis McWilliam gave us a warm welcome and arranged with
a neighbour for us to leave the van in his front garden. The
horses had to be led away to a field at the other end of the
town. Tony sat astride Jack bare backed, while I followed
with Bill. A man shouted to us, " Is it a Buffalo Bill show
you've got? " He seemed disappointed when we told him we

165

were merely a couple of ' tinks,' and I doubt if he believed us. So at last, very weary after one of the most exhausting days we had experienced, we turned in to sleep.

I made a sketch of the pretty little church at Forres, and also visited Elgin in order t o draw the only pre-Reformation Franciscan friary in Great Britain which has been restored to Catholic worship. Greyfriars, Elgin, was desecrated in the 16th century, its buildings being allowed to fall into ruin. About fifty years ago they were purchased by the Marquis of Bute, who restored them at great expense. They are now occupied by the Sisters of Mercy. The lovely 14th century church was re-opened on St. Francis Day, 1898. The interior, with its oak rood screen dividing the nave from the choir, is in perfect taste. The painted crucifix which surmounts it is copied from the miraculous crucifix preserved in St. Clare's Convent, Assisi. On the left of the screen is an altar, whose reredos depicts saints of the Order of Mercy. On the right is a reredos with five Franciscan saints. On the north wall of the sanctuary is a fine example of a typical pre-Reformation ' Sacrament House,' or aumbry, in which the Blessed Sacrament used to be reserved in the Middle Ages throughout Scotland. Greyfriars, Elgin, is a sanctuary of which Scottish Catholics may well be proud. Nowhere else in the country can one visualise what its Catholic churches must have been like before John Knox and his followers did their best to destroy the ' superstitious idolatry' of the ' Scarlet Woman ' of the Apocalypse.

I wrote up these notes last night while sitting in the van after tea the last evening we spent at Forres. The following morning we got away about 10.30. No startling events happened on the road. We crossed Hardmoor, the ' blasted heath ' where Macbeth and Banquo met the witches, but saw no sign of them on this bright June day under a cloudless sky. We stopped for lunch outside Nairn, and found camping ground at a farm close to the sea shore within a couple of miles of Inverness, to which we were directed by one of those ever-helpful A.A. scouts, who are seldom too proud to come to our aid, just as if we were touring in a luxurious motor trailer instead of a disreputable old gipsy van.

Some real gipsies—or more correctly tinkers—were camping in a small tent near the farm. They made friends with us and were glad of a present of coal and cigarettes. The farmer's wife told us that she made quite a good profit from campers during the summer months. In fact this is the case in all parts of Great Britain. Farmers have begun to realise that caravans and hikers are worth encouraging.

We had the usual trouble with Jack on leaving the farm. He refused to stand still and had to be chased round the yard. Finally we got away about 9.30 and made for Inverness. We crossed the suspension bridge and stopped in front of the Catholic church where my old friend, the late Canon Shaw, who, being country born and bred, came out to have a look at the horses whose good qualities he knew how to appreciate.

On our way through the streets a shabbily dressed old man stopped Tony and said he would give a good price for the ' big horse '—meaning Bill. " No," shouted Tony. " I don't want to sell him." " Why you don't need two horses," said the man. " I know, cos I've driven hundreds of miles in a van like yours. I'll give you fifteen pounds down if you'll sell." But Tony was not moved by this unexpected offer from the disreputable looking gentleman, whose clothes did not lead one to suppose that he had so much money to spend on a horse.

Leaving Tony to talk to Canon Shaw and his curate I re-crossed the river to make a sketch of the church. There is not much left to-day in the capital of the Highlands to remind one that St. Columba said Mass here in the 6th century. Presbyterian Kirks—Established, ' Free,' and of other species, also an Episcopalian Cathedral, have taken the place of friaries and convents. Only the name ' Greyfriars ' remains as witness of

St. Mary's, Inverness.

the flourishing Catholic life of Inverness before the Reformation. After the introduction of Calvinism in the 16th century it is doubtful if Mass was ever said here until 1810, when a room was obtained in which a few Catholics, mostly from Strathglass, used to meet for worship. They were looked after by the priest from Eskadale.

The present church was opened in 1837. Funds for its erection were collected by the Rev. Terence Maguire, who had been appointed to Inverness ten years before. It was an Irishman who had brought the Catholic Faith to Inverness in the 6th century. Another Irishman restored it thirteen hundred years later. The exterior of St. Mary's Church still remains as an unspoilt and most interesting example of the early Gothic Revival. But one regrets that the ' elegantly painted cornices and gilt ceiling ' to which a contemporary writer refers have been removed. Yet in spite of its altar decked out with wedding cake-like crockets and pinnacles in the characteristic Peter Paul Pugin manner, the interior still retains a pleasant feeling of ' Early Victorianism.'

We said good-bye to Canon Shaw and drove on towards Clachnaharry. We had not gone very far when the would-be purchaser of the horse caught up with us. He saluted me and said : " Sir, your man tells me he'll sell the big horse. I'll wait until you get back to England. Fifteen pound, and the money down. I'll put it right into your hand. Your humble servant, William Ross."

He gave me his address and I said I would write to him later on if I wanted to sell Bill. It seemed strange that we get so many offers to buy our horses in Scotland. Perhaps it is due to the universal Clydesdale horse all over the country. No doubt there are many advantages in a smaller and less powerful beast for certain jobs.

We stopped for lunch just beyond Moniack Castle. An inquisitive policeman interrupted our meal and wanted to know all about our business. Anything that suggests a tinker always seems to rouse the suspicions of a Scottish policeman. I feel sorry for our fellow vagrants whose life must be none too easy.

So on again to Lovat Bridge. We turned left here, and crossing the river near the Falls of Kilmorack, and took a rough road which climbed up over a hill, then descended once more into the valley. On our right lay Eilean Aigas, at that time rented by Mr. Compton Mackenzie, who was making preparations to migrate to his new home on the Isle of Barra. We nearly lost the chimney on this road, for the branches of the trees hung down very low. It was always difficult for the driver to calculate just how much room there was to spare, if indeed he had time to take his mind off the horses. So quite often I had to give warning, " Look out for the chimney! Branches ahead! "

The sun was sinking down behind the mountains; the trees casting long shadows across the road, when we drew up besides the church at Eskadale, where Fr. Geddes soon made us feel at home. The beauty of the landscape was somewhat spoilt by the plague of midges from whose attack it was impossible to escape, except by shutting all the windows in the van, or by smoking hard. We little knew how much we should have to endure from midges and clegs during the next few weeks. This was merely the beginning of our purgatory.

We spent a quiet week-end in Eskadale. The caravan was parked on the side of a road which led through the woods, and from our doorstep we could look out over the river. Neither Tony nor myself will forget the characteristic ' Highland welcome' we received from Fr. Geddes, the kind and genial parish priest.

The lower end of Strathglass has always remained a Catholic oasis in the midst of a Presbyterian desert, mainly due to the loyalty of the Chisholms and Frasers to the Old Religion. There are records of ' Popish chapels ' in different parts of Strathglass throughout the 18th century. The present church at Eskadale was built by Lord Lovat in 1826, " on a scale of grandeur hitherto unknown in the Highlands," to quote a

St. Mary's, Eskadale.

contemporary writer. I was surprised to see such massive 'Norman' columns separating the nave from the aisles, and must confess that I found the primitive low-backed benches more conducive to penance than comfort when occupying one of them at Mass on Sunday morning. Lord Lovat and his family are more fortunate than their dependents. They occupy armchairs in a raised pew at the back of the church as if to emphasise their exalted station in the social hierarchy.

Fr. Geddes pointed out to us the graves of seven priests in the churchyard, where also lie the two brothers Sobieski-Stuart, who claimed descent from 'Bonnie Prince Charlie.'

THIRTEEN

Marydale—Fort Augustus—Roybridge—the pedlar—
Glenfinnan—Fort William.

The weather had been very kind to us for the past fortnight and we had no rain to speak of until we reached Fort Augustus. It certainly made driving more enjoyable, on the other hand we should have been glad if the heat had not been so exhausting. And both Jack and Bill would have agreed with these sentiments when, covered in sweat, or with lathered bodies, they plodded along the roads.

It was nearly midday that Monday morning when we left Eskadale. The road surface was very rough and I was shaken to bits inside the van where I was trying to keep a saucepan from falling off the Primus stove. On such occasions the only thing to do is to put the stove inside a pail and stand it firmly on the floor.

We passed many ruined crofts; a reminder of the great eviction which in 1801 cleared Strathglass of most of its inhabitants. That year 8,000 persons from Scotland emigrated to Nova Scotia. In fact no less than between three and four thousand crofters were driven out the glen by Mrs. Elizabeth Chisholm. She seems to have inherited from her mother, Mrs. Duncan Macdonnel of Glengarry, a passion for evicting tenants. The latter carried on the same wholesale policy on her own estates. The aim of some of these Highland liards at that period was to completely depopulate their lands and turn them into sheep farms. One is glad to record that Lord Lovat, on hearing of the harsh proceedings of his neighbour, offered to give up one of his own big farms and divide it up among the evicted crofters from the Chisholm estates. This took place in 1830. By 1880 Strathglass—to quote from

173

Mackenzie's *Highland Clearances*—had become "a perfect wilderness" in which lived " no less than three colonels, one major, three captains, three lieutenants, seven ensigns, one bishop, and fifteen priests." The same writer informs us that " the result of the Strathglass evictions was that only two of the native stock remained in possession of an inch of land on the estate of Chisholm." Yet time had its revenge for all the evicting Chisholms; and their offspring disappeared, and in 1880 there was not a human being in Strathglass descended from the chief, or from the Lowland farmers who were mainly responsible for evicting the native population.

We crossed the river Beauly at Struy and lunched on the roadside. A mile or so beyond Struy a woman came out of a cottage and beckoned to me, with a smile on her face. "Would you like a glass of milk? " she asked. Rather surprised at this unexpected offer, and feeling very thirsty, I gratefully accepted. She went into the house and presently returned with two glasses of rich creamy milk for Tony and myself. " I saw you at Mass yesterday," she explained. " I heard you would be passing this way, and I've been on the look out for the caravan all the morning."

We drank the milk and handed back the empty glasses. " I read the *Universe* every week," our kind hostess went on to explain, " so you see I know all about you and your horses. What a long way you have come since you left the south of England. May God and Our Lady protect you."

We shook hands with this supporter of the Catholic press, and, bidding her farewell, continued our journey. She waved to us until we were out of sight. " Seems to me you've got friends wherever we go," remarked Tony. " It's a great thing being the ' Pilgrim Artist ' when it means free drinks on a hot afternoon."

Some distance before we reached Invercannich we noticed the tower of the Catholic church rising up out the trees. We turned left at the cross roads and were glad to meet Fr. Colin

Macdonald, who had entertained us at Fetternear about three weeks earlier. Since then he had ' flitted ' to his new parish. A convenient place for the caravan was selected on level ground behind the church. I mention ' level ground ' for if by chance there happened to be the least slope in any direction, the cupboard doors are inclined to fly open unless firmly locked. And what is even more inconvenient, one cannot keep pots and pans from slipping off the stove. So you see how careful we have to be to find a level base for the van when stopping in any place.

Few Highland churches can equal Marydale for beauty of situation. It stands besides a river in the midst of a wooded glen with mountains rising up on either side. I climbed up on to a rocky bank to make a sketch, but it was not easy to convey the character of the landscape in pen and ink line, for its charm lies rather in the colour.

Presbyterianism failed to gain many adherents in Strathglass in spite of the fact that there does not seem to have been any resident priests here before the end of the 17th century. After the conversion of Colin Chisholm of Knockfin about that date two chapels were built, and henceforth Strathglass was seldom without priests, two of whom, John and Aeneas Chisholm, became Vicars Apostolic of the Highland District.

The present church at Marydale dates from 1868. It was designed by Joseph Hansom and is a simple Gothic structure. As I have already explained, owing to the eviction of most of the crofters from Strathglass about a hundred years ago there are not many people left here to-day, except a few gamekeepers and other families who are employed on the estates. Strathglass has become the preserve of sportsmen, most of whom seldom reside here for more than two or three months in the year. It is sad to relate that this migration is still going on. In these days it becomes increasingly difficult for the younger generation in these Highland glens to earn even a bare living, for there is no work for them. And so economic pressure drives

175

Our Lady and St. Bean, Marydale, Strathglass.

them away from home even more ruthlessly than did the lairds when they decided it would be more profitable to themselves to turn crofts into sheep grazing, and when this failed into deer forests.

We decided to make an early start the following morning, and turned out of bed soon after 5 a.m. An hour later we were on the road. There was a long stiff climb after leaving Glen Cannich. The horses were put in traces and managed the hill without any bother. But by the time they reached the top their flanks were all lathered, as if covered in soap suds, so we gave them a well deserved rest before going on.

Twelve miles of gradual descent through Glen Urquhart brought us to Drumnadrochit—and Loch Ness. Tony was eager for a sight of The MONSTER—but he did not choose to put in an appearance in spite of a sharp look out, especially when we were above Castle Urquhart near which he has been spotted more than once.

Of the beauty of that view over the still waters of Loch Ness it is waste of words to attempt a description. Surely the road from Inverness to Fort Augustus must take first prize for any similar length of road in Great Britain? And what a glorious road for a motorist with its easy gradients, perfect surface, and great breadth. Jack and Bill strode up and down its almost imperceptible slopes as if they were walking on a dead level. Driving on such a road was so easy that Tony had no fear that I could do any harm, so allowed me to take the reins for several hours that afternoon. We stopped opposite Foyers and had a pleasant picnic lunch.

The road keeps close to the Loch all the way to Fort Augustus, a distance of nearly twenty-four miles. Sometimes it is on the level of the water, then it climbs up on to a cliff, in places about 100 feet above the shore. So the views are constantly changing every few minutes.

The abbey clock was chiming seven as we entered Fort Augustus and crossed the bridges over the Caledonian Canal and river Ness. We have covered nearly 34 miles since the morning and the horses have done their duty like heroes. Never have they pulled so well. But a few days rest will do them good.

The caravan has found a resting place in a yard outside the abbey gates, while Jack and Bill are allowed to roam in one of the school playing fields.

Having known Fort Augustus Abbey and its community for nearly twenty years it is difficult for me to write about either from an impartial point of view. It is rather like attempting to describe one's own home and relations. But for those who have not been so fortunate as myself I will try to give a brief account of the monastery and its history.

The community can proudly claim continuity with the two ancient Scottish monasteries of Ratisbon in Bavaria and Lambspring in Hanover, both of which were supressed over a century ago. It was Lord Lovat who actually founded the present monastery in 1870 when he handed over the old fort, erected in 1729 by the English military authorities, to the Anglo-Benedictine Congregation. Another benefactor was the Marquis of Bute, who gave generous financial support. The first superior was Dom Jerome Vaughan, brother of Cardinal Vaughan.

The 18th century barracks, governor's house, and courtyard might have been adapted for monastic purposes, but in 1876 it would have been considered indecent to house a Benedictine community in buildings which were not definitely ' Gothic.' So Joseph Hansom and Peter Paul Pugin were called in to direct the demolition of the old fort. On its site they erected the guest house (this portion of the buildings is not so modern as it looks, for the architect merely disguised the original guard house with a Gothic facing!), college, monastery and cloisters in the most elaborate style of Decorated Gothic. Only the foundations of the church and two chapels were completed. In 1917 the choir was built, from the designs of Reginald Fairlie. A corrugated iron nave and sanctuary have contined

St. Benedict's Abbey, Fort Augustus.

to be somewhat of an eyesore for the past eighteen years, and funds are still lacking to replace them and finish the church.

For the first few years of its existence the community remained part of the Anglo-Benedictine Congregation. But in 1882 it became an independent house, directly subject to the Holy See and raised to the status of an abbey. In 1910 it was reunited to the Anglo-Benedictine Congregation.

If you want to read the impressions of an outsider on life at Fort Augustus Abbey I would refer you to H. V. Morton's *In Search of Scotland*. As I have said already I know and love the place too intimately to condense into a few pages all that I should like to say.

We had our meals at the guests' table in the monastic refectory during the five days spent at Fort Augustus. This gave me a rest from cooking. Tony as usual made friends with everybody, and soon became at home in the abbey. One day he donned full Highland costume (borrowed from one of the men who worked in the gardens). It happened to fit him quite well. He posed to have several photographs taken, and when they were printed sent the results to his family in Yorkshire to show them that he had ' gone native.' I told him he looked like Harry Lauder. But he did not venture to go ' roaming in the gloaming ' in this garb.

Most of the community came to inspect the caravan, including the Abbot and the lay brothers. The latter were particularly interested in all our domestic arrangements.

Tony was always hoping he would see the Monster before we left Fort Augustus, but he gazed at Loch Ness in vain. There was an American journalist also on the look out for ' copy ' for her paper, and she was getting very indignant that her visit had been merely a waste of time. I myself was too busy making drawings of the monastery and church to bother about ' monsters,' and when these were completed, we were ready to set off again.

We left Fort Augustus on the morning of July 2nd. We

stopped for lunch beside Loch Lochy, just beyond Laggan. The first glimpse of Ben Nevis, three hours later, was an excuse to make another halt for tea. Near Spean Bridge we passed several groups of tinkers, camping by the roadside. Like most of the present generation of Scottish tinkers they had abandoned their horses and carts in favour of second-hand motor-cars. And I am not surprised, for every day it becomes more difficult to travel with horses as we ourselves had begun to realise. For one thing the modern roads are made for motor traffic, and in England at any rate, as Tony has so often related in *The Brown Caravan,* their smooth surface affords no grip to a horse's hoofs. Then again one may go for miles and never come across a blacksmith; even corn merchants and saddlers are far less numerous than ten years ago. Finally it is difficult to find grazing for horses. One cannot let them wander on the roads owing to the traffic; and nearly every bit of common land now has a notice put up ' No camping here!' Unless one happens to find a friendly farmer with a field available one is at a loss to know what to do with horses; no longer are there stables at the hotels and wayside inns, for they have been transformed into garages. So the gipsies and tinkers are being forced to conform to the spirit of the age, and before long it will be difficult to find one who has not got an old car instead of horses as a means of conveyance. But they have not yet given up those peculiar shaped tents, which are their traditional home; a relic which has come down through many centuries, even before they first crossed into Europe from Central Asia. The picturesque gipsy caravan is, so I believe, a comparatively modern innovation. Until about a century ago both English gipsies and Scottish tinkers travelled about with carts in which all their possessions were packed away, including the tents in which they lived, even during the winter.

We camped that night beside the church at Roybridge, an attractive little building designed by Reginald Fairlie. Its

181

austerely simple exterior seems to fit in with the character of the landscape, and does not try to compete with the towering mass of Ben Nevis and its neighbouring mountains of which a fine view can be had at this spot. The district of Lochaber has always remained Catholic since the Reformation, and the teachings of Knox and Calvin failed to take root here. Throughout the 17th and 18th centuries there were missionary priests stationed in Lochaber. Mass was generally said in barns or in the open-air, and it was not until about 150 years ago that a permanent chapel was built. This was little better than a thatched hovel. In 1826 a more decent structure was erected at Bun Roy, which was in use until 1929 when it was replaced by the present church, dedicated to St. Margaret,

We left Roybridge after breakfast. On passing through Spean Bridge, a woman spoke to me, being curious to know who we were and where we came from. " Fancy travelling all the way from Yorkshire in that affair!," she remarked, as if doubting the truth of the statement. She told us she had a son working on a farm in Sussex and a daughter in service in London. " There's no work to be got in these parts," she explained. " So most of the young folk have to go away after they leave school."

Such is the story one hears almost everywhere in the Highlands. It is sad to realise that this steady migration southwards cannot be checked. But what can be done when almost every attempt to start industries in the Highlands is obstructed by the sentimental protests of wealthy landlords who complain that factory buildings, electric pylons, or workmens' cottages will ruin the ' amenities ' of the scenery, or the great open spaces of ' Caledonia stern and wild '? A large number of those who are most opposed to Highland development schemes seldom reside on their sporting estates for more than a few months in the year. Tourist traffic comes to an end in September and only starts in July, so for the remaining nine months the Highlands are little better than a silent and empty desert.

Evidences of the wish to exploit the summer tourists were apparent on every side in this district. Many of the cottages and crofts advertised that they could provide ' Night Accommodation ' or ' Bed and Breakfast.' Although it was only the first week in July we met quite a number of motor caravans and trailers. Bare-kneed hikers, male and female, with heavy ruck-sacks on their shoulders, were becoming more and more frequent. When passing by McDonald's ' Long John Distillery ' we nearly came to grief. Some men came out and started rolling empty casks along the road. Jack and Bill took fright. If Tony had not got hold of the reins in time, for I happened to be driving, I think the caravan would have crashed into the side of Lochy Bridge.

We stopped at Banavie to watch a drifter going through the eleven locks (' Neptune's Staircase ') at the entrance to the Caledonian Canal; a slow and laborious process.

Finding a shady spot on the shore of Loch Eil where there was good grass upon which the horses could graze without fear of traffic, we decided to stop for lunch. The place could not have been more attractive, but we had not reckoned with winged visitors in the shape of clegs, or horse flies, which for the first time attacked us.

A mile or two beyond, having continued our slow progress on that hot afternoon, we came up to a man who was plodding along the road, with a large pack on his back. We asked him if he would like a lift, and he willingly accepted; taking his seat on the step beside Tony, and stowing away his pack and wicker basket in the van.

" You're a long way from home," he remarked, having noticed ' Ugthorpe, Yorkshire,' painted on the side of the van. He explained to us that he was a pedler, and showed us the contents of his basket—needles, pins, cotton, boot laces, and wool. Another smaller case contained all his personal needs—a change of clothes, razor, etc. He also carried a little tent, in which, so he told us, he often slept when other accommodation could not be found. He hailed from Sheffield and his name was William Mellor.

183

" There isn't many North Country folk up here," he said. " It's good to meet another Yorkshireman."

He hadn't forgotten how to speak West Riding dialect, but it was mixed up with a number of words and phrases picked up in Scotland. He told us he had travelled all over England, especially in the southern counties, but knew Yorkshire and Lancashire best of all. His clothes were worn, but of good material and well cut. Most likely he had bought them second-hand. His thick black trousers, heavy jacket, worsted socks and stout boots were not exactly the ideal costume when tramping along the road on a hot afternoon in July.

He said that in recent years he had remained in Scotland, finding that there was more money to be made in the remote districts of the West Highlands. The glens and straths of Argyllshire, Inverness-shire, Ross and Cromarty provided good business. But the Isle of Skye was the most profitable.

The pedler told us that he went south during the winter months, making Paisley or Campbeltown his headquarters. He ordered his goods from a wholesale firm in Glasgow and had them sent on whenever his stock ran low.

" By gum! " he remarked, mopping his forehead, " it's gey warm walking. It isn't many pairs of horses on the roads you see nowadays. Where are you making for to-night? I'm going to Mallaig." I said that we hoped to reach Glenfinnan, but would go no further.

" Just as well," he replied. " You'll find the road very bad, only loose stones and full of ruts. Have you met any ' tinks ' on your travels? " " Yes, I answered. " Generally quite friendly too." " Give 'em a wide berth is my advice. They'll pinch anything they can lay hands on. It's best to keep out of their way. You see, at peddling on the roads they have me beat. Me on my own ain't a chance in a village. Nine or ten ' tinks ' all going to different houses is a mug's game on the beaten track. Another thing, they're always cadging. As soon as they camp, off they go; the kids to a croft or cottages, begging milk, eggs, bread—anything in fact."

I asked Mellor why so few gipsies and tinkers in Scotland had vans and why they have preferred to push prams or travel about with small carts. "These travellers ain't real gipsies," he explained. "They're what I call cuckoo-birds, just come out in the summer and hole up in the winter. They ain't like the English gipsies. Not half as good either. They're always on the road."

I ventured to disagree with his views on the Scottish tinkers, pointing out that in several instances we had found them only too ready to help us, mentioning the night we had spent in their company at Glamis.

I asked him what made him take up peddling as a means of earning a living. "I started off after the War. I used to work on farms, but didn't feel I wanted to go back to that sort of life. So I began by buying winkles in large quantities; boiled them, and then sold them at 2d. a bag. Folk like winkles in Lancashire, and I was living in Preston at that time. I made quite a good profit. Then I tried peddling. But there were too many Woolworths in Lancashire. Laces could never make more than a penny, an' besides that, folks in towns seem to either pity a poor pedler, or else slam the door in his face. A pedler in England is treated worse than a tramp. That's why I came to Scotland."

I enquired if he had always been on his own or if he had ever had a partner. I wondered if he ever felt lonely. "Aye! Odd times I do," he answered with a smile. "But you see not many chaps will stick this kind of life; it's too hard for them. I've tried several, but they didn't stay long and then cleared off. All right for a change, but peddling isn't every man's job."

I could well realise it from what I had learnt that afternoon. But it was good to meet a man of this type who valued his independence more than the comforts of ordinary civilised life. I suggested that he might care to travel with us for a week or two, for he would have been an interesting companion. But he declined the offer, saying that he had his regular round among the farms and crofts away north in Knoydart, and could not stick to the high roads.

After jogging along for some four or five miles we stopped for tea. The pedler looked rather disdainfully at our Primus stove, and explained just how he lit a fire, and how much better it was than any sort of stove. After tea we had a smoke, and I was sorry when our welcome visitor said he must be leaving us. He slung his pack on to his shoulder, seized his heavily laden basket, and set off over a path among the heather in the direction of a lonely croft. That was the last we saw of William Mellor, the Yorkshire pedler. I have often wondered since that day if he is still tramping through the West Highlands and if we shall ever meet again.

As we had been warned the road soon became very narrow and the surface incredibly bad soon after we left the shores of Loch Eil. It got worse and worse as we proceeded westwards, and I began to fear for the safety of the van as it bumped and jolted over the loose stones; the wheels sometimes sticking in the deep ruts. And yet this road was marked on the map as a ' first class ' one !

" This is what comes of trusting your beastly maps! " remarked Tony. " Why on earth you want to bring me to a God-forsaken spot like this, I'm blessed if I know! " And well might he protest, for in addition to the awful road the horses were being ravaged by hordes of clegs, who were drawing blood from their exposed flanks.

I realised that we should never be able to reach Glenfinnan that night, where I had made arrangements for grazing the horses in a field belonging to the hotel proprietor. So about 7 p.m. I told Tony to turn on to a bit of grass beside the road where the caravan would not be in the way of the traffic. After some search we managed to find ground which was not boggy and here we tethered Jack and Bill to the heavy iron spikes which we had brought with us in case of an emergency like this.

Neither of us will ever forget that night. The weather was close and sultry. We decided to sleep in the tent which we pitched among the heather, collecting enough bracken to make a fairly soft bed. But having made ourselves comfortable and settled down to sleep, we realised that we were not the only occupants of the tent. Midges stung us on our faces, arms, and hands. About midnight we could endure them no longer. We made a hasty retreat for the interior of the caravan. But it was now raining and we got soaked while falling about in the deep heather, each of us laden with pillows and blankets. It was too dark to see clearly where we were going.

Having got to bed again and fallen asleep, an hour later we were awakened by the piercing whinny of a horse. Tony hastily dressed himself, and discovered that Jack had broken loose and was wandering about among the boggy ground. After some trouble he was captured and re-tethered to the stake. We hoped that this would be the last of our trials, and once more turned in to get some sleep.

After breakfast the following morning I walked on to Glenfinnan, about two miles beyond where we had spent the night. Famous in history as the spot where the Marquis of Tullibardine raised the standard of 'Bonnie Prince Charlie' in 1745, Glenfinnan (like most of the district of Moydart) has always remained Catholic since the Reformation. Until 1874 the nearest places of worship were at Glenuig, at the lower end of Loch Shiel, and Arisaig, both of them about fifteen miles away.

I found the modern church, a pretty little Gothic structure designed by Edward Pugin, hidden away on a wooded site commanding a beautiful view of Loch Shiel. It is a place of sad pathetic memories to anyone who is interested in the history of the Stuarts. I noticed a tablet on the walls put up in memory of the 'Young Pretender,' and I recalled having read that at the opening of this church some fifty years ago, the same pipes were played which had echoed through the glens at

St. Mary and St. Finnan, Glenfinnan.

that historic gathering of the clans in this very spot.   And
what is more curious it happened to be the anniversary of that
fateful event.

We started to retrace our steps along the rough road late in
the afternoon, having decided that it was too hot to make it
worth while starting earlier.   The clegs were just as murderous
in their attacks as on the previous day.   I got a brain wave
and tried the experiment of pinning sheets round the horses.
They looked a strange sight thus dressed up.   But the sheets
would not stay put, and got rucked up as the horses moved
along.   So after a few miles I took them off again.

It was too late to make Fort William that night, so we
found a camp site at Fassfern House, where Prince Charlie
stopped for four days after raising his standard at Glenfinnan.
A lovely spot with glorious views over the still waters of Loch
Eil and the towering mass of Ben Nevis in the distance.

The following morning we continued our journey to Banavie,
recrossing Lochy Bridge without the horses being alarmed at
any more empty whisky casks.

The list of addresses printed in the Camping Club's Handbook, of which I had thought it might be useful to be a
member, had generally proved of little or no service.   Few of
the recommended farms or camp sites made any provision for
horses.   But here was an exception.   On a notice board we
read the invitation, ' Pick your own site if attendant is absent.'
Seeing nobody about on this field next to the distillery, we
obeyed the injunctions, and chose the most convenient corner
we could find where the ground was level.

Later on the owner of the field turned up, an ex-soldier—
late Gordon Highlanders—with whom we had some interesting
talks that afternoon and evening.   Tony was feeling quite stiff
and sore after all the bumping and shaking he had endured
on that rough road to and from Glenfinnan.   So he was glad

to spend a lazy (?) afternoon, sitting on the shady side of the caravan, cleaning harness.

I went into Fort William to sketch Reginald Fairlie's new church; a most impressive structure with its square tower at the east end above the sanctuary. I greatly admired the wrought iron baldachino over the High Altar, which struck a quite original note.

FOURTEEN

Ballachulish—Glencoe—Loch Lomond—Drymen—
Lennoxtown—the Irish in Scotland.

We were awake soon after 5 a.m. and by 6.30 were driving through the still empty streets of Fort William, where all the inhabitants appeared to be still in bed.   Four miles beyond the town we stopped for breakfast on the shores of Loch Linnhe; a delightful spot, with a wide view of the sea and mountains.

As the morning wore on the heat became more intense.   We were certainly ' enjoying ' real summer weather in the West Highlands.   Clegs still followed us, and it seemed impossible to find any way to prevent them fastening themselves on the horses and sticking there until they had gorged themselves with blood.   I tried walking beside the horses and flicking off the clegs with an old slipper.   But others soon replaced them.

I peeped into the little Episcopalian church at Onich, which seemed to be conducted on extremely ritualistic lines.   Few Catholic churches in the Highlands can compete with St. Bride's, Onich, as regards the externals of worship.   They are generally bare and simple in the decorations.

It was annoying that we could not make use of the ferry at North Ballachulish, but we were afraid there would be trouble with the horses who generally took fright at anything unusual of this sort.   Our destination lay across the water, not more than a mile from the ferry.   But to reach it we had to cover nearly twenty miles right round the top end of Loch Leven. The road proved to be one of those switchback affairs with nasty steep banks.

The heat was overpowering, the glassy water of the loch lay unruffled by even the least trace of a breeze.   We were thankful to reach Kinlochleven and turn eastwards again on the opposite side of the loch. The village, with its aluminium works and rows of workmen's cottages, is unlike any other place in the Highlands. I had often heard it described as a 'blot on the landscape,' but personally I was glad to find evidences of some kind of activity in the midst of so much useless and unprofitable desolation.

From Kinlochleven we took the fine new road made by German prisoners during the War. Before this the only way of access was from the north. We stopped for tea where there was a magnificent view over the Loch with some of the highest and most precipitous mountains in Scotland towering up above us on either side of the deep valley. We did not arrive at East Ballachulish until after 9 o'clock, feeling desperately weary after nearly fifteen hours on the move, not to mention the heat.

East Ballachulish is a curious little village in the midst of slate quarries. On one side is Loch Leven, and steep mountains rise up behind it. The mission is always referred to as Glencoe, and I had had no idea that the Catholic church is situated nearly two miles from the lower end of the glen itself until I asked the way from a man we met on the road.

It would seem that the infamous massacre of Glencoe, which took place in 1692, was largely due to religious motives, for the Macdonalds of Glencoe were Catholics and hated by the Presbyterian Campbells of Glen Lyon. Despite this brutal massacre the Faith managed to survive in Glencoe. In 1836, when the present church was erected at East Ballachulish, the congregation numbered about 100. I liked this homely little church. It cannot claim any architectural interest, but it is in keeping with its surroundings which is even more important.

I noticed an unusual feature; the Gaelic inscriptions beneath the Stations of the Cross, the only instance which I can recall in Scotland. In the Outer Isles the sermons are always preached in Gaelic and in some places evening devotions are conducted in this language. But it is become less common in

8.7.1934

P.F. ANSON

St. Mun's, Glencoe.

churches on the mainland, for most of the congregations can understand English.

In fact Gaelic is dying, in spite of valiant efforts to preserve it. With the advent of the radio into the most remote districts of the Highlands I fear it will be even harder to induce the next generation to converse in the language of their ancestors, unless, as in Ireland, definite steps are taken by the authorities to make Gaelic compulsory for all those who are employed in public services.

We spent a quiet week-end at East Ballachulish. Tony found much to interest him in watching sheep being clipped. Six men were kept hard at work shearing. The average time spent on each sheep was eight minutes. The work was carried on to the accompaniment of rapid conversation in Gaelic.

The weather remained so hot that we came to the conclusion that we would travel by night. So we did not leave Ballachulish until 6.30 p.m. Neither Tony nor myself will ever forget that journey through Glencoe. One hears complaints that the magnificent new road has ' spoilt ' the character of the glen by making it accessible to motor buses and char-a-bancs. But for ourselves we were more than grateful to the engineers who were responsible for the easy gradients and splendid surface. Jack and Bill marched along side by side, apparently with no extra strain or effort. They did not need a rest until they had climbed the thousand feet from the shore of Leven. I pointed out to Tony the various points of interest; Loch Triochcan on our right beside whose Kelpic-haunted waters the poet Ossian is said to have been born; the ' Three Sisters,' whose jagged peaks—Aonach-Dubh, Gearr-Aonach, and Ben Fhada —rose up precipitously on our left.

As the rays of the setting sun cast longer and longer shadows, the sun itself at last disappearing behind the mountains, the glen became more and more beautiful. There was very little traffic on the road at this hour, and hardly any motors

194

disturbed the peacefulness of the scene.

We reached the watershed about 10 o'clock and stopped for a late supper, also to admire the views, both behind and ahead of us. To the east lay the rolling expanse of Rannoch Moor; bogs and small lochs. To the west Glencoe itself, with the road twisting down and down until it changed from a white ribbon into a faint wavy line, almost invisible in the increasing twilight. The mountains stood out like a deep blue silhouette against a sky of rosy orange; the loftiest of them all, Buchaille Etive Mor—" the shepherd of Elive "—keeping silent watch over the glen.

We moved on again across the moor. Even at midnight it was not really dark, and a strange ghostly half-twilight provided sufficient illumination to make our lamps almost needless for the purpose of driving. Mile after mile we moved on across the monotonous expanse of moor and bog. During the early hours of the morning before the first sign of dawn appeared in the east, mist rose up from stagnant pools, giving the scene an even more eerie look; forming ghost-like shapes that might have been the spirits of the dead watching our progress, and wondering who we were to disturb their nocturnal communings. A curious smell—difficult to define— rose up from the bogs, rather like a damp Harris tweed, but not so pleasant. The horses plodded on, the clop-clop of their eight hoofs doing a sort of tap-dance on the concrete surface of the road to the accompaniment of Tony's whistling. Sometimes they would shy at an invisible terror—heard by their keen ears but not by their driver. We could understand better why they took fright at the stark looking concrete bridges across which we rumbled at intervals. The air became quite chilly and we were glad of our coats.

About two o'clock Tony told me to lie down and get a sleep. But sleep refused to come. I kept on peeping out of the little window above the bed to see where we had got to. Moreover, the hard concrete surface of the road did not help to induce sleep. The wheels seemed to make more noise than usual. I lay still, and above their continuous rumble could hear the driver whistling, or occasionally bursting into song.

It was broad daylight by the time we arrived at Loch Tulla, although only 4 o'clock. Here we stopped for breakfast, a cup of hot coffee being very welcome after our long vigil. It was a curious experience to be picnicking at this unusual hour.

We moved on again, and about 7 a.m. felt we had come far enough, and anxious to find a convenient place where we could spend the rest of the day. But grazing for the horses was not easy to discover in this land of moor and bog. We kept a sharp look out on either side of the road, but it was some time before we saw any suitable spot. At last we came in sight of a river at a short distance to the left of the road. Here there was quite good grass, even if broken up with rough and boggy patches. So we turned into a stone quarry, unharnessed the horses, led them down the bank and staked them out to graze.

We ourselves, now feeling very tired, lay down to sleep. But as the sun rose the heat inside the caravan became so over-powering, that after an hour or two, we could stand it no longer, and decided to go down to the river bank, where there were some trees. Here we found welcome shade from the sun, and here we lazed for the rest of the day. At intervals we paddled in the ice cold water and splashed our heads. But clegs, and later on midges, were a constant plague. I cannot say that we enjoyed ourselves, and began to wish we were miles away from the Highlands. Both of us were inclined to be ' nervy ' and argumentative; the effect of overtiredness, and we were glad when it was cool enough to return to the caravan and go to bed.

We set the alarum clock for 4 o'clock, and were off again about three-quarters of an hour later. There was a long pull up to the watershed between the Atlantic and the North Sea. Having risen to a level of about 1,050 feet we entered Perth-shire, which we had left behind at Meigle nearly six weeks ago.

At Crianlarich we stopped at the post office to see if there were any letters for us. A few miles further on, while descending the steep road through Glen Falloch, Jack pulled one of his hind shoes off. So we had to stop while Tony took out his blacksmith's tools and repaired the damage. I often wondered what I should have done in such crises if my companion had not been a blacksmith, in addition to possessing an intimate knowledge of horses from other points of view.

The shoe having been nailed on again we resumed our journey and did not stop until we arrived at the upper end of Loch Lomond. Here we found a delightfully shady spot just beyond Ardlui, well away from the road, where there was good grazing for the horses. While eating our dinner beneath the so-called ' Pilgrims Rock ' a man came up to us and began to talk. We learnt that he had been in the Canadian Mounted Police at one time.

" I love horses," he said. " I would give anything to have one again. Nowadays I try to earn a living by doing pen and ink portraits. I live in Kent, and came up here by car with my wife. We camp out at nights." He gazed at Jack and Bill with a covetous look in his eyes. They were standing still in the shade of a rock and made a pretty picture. " Well I must be getting off. I do envy you two chaps. So long ! "

After a good rest and feeling much refreshed, we set off again late in the afternoon when it was beginning to get cooler. About 9.30 p.m. we drove into Tarbet where it was only after much search that I managed to find camping ground. Tarbet seemed to be overrun with tourists and the inhabitants didn't seem to like the look of us. We weren't quite up to the ' class ' they are used to !

We awoke to find that it had been raining during the night, and that the ground was still wet. Soon after 6 o'clock we had left Tarbet and its tourists still reposing in their beds, and were jogging along beside the Loch.

The Annual Glasgow ' Fair Week ' had begun, and it

appeared that the greater number of the inhabitants of that city had decided to spend their holidays on the ' bonny banks of Loch Lomond.' Never had I realised there could be such a congestion of tents, caravans, and trailers, for there was scarcely a bit of vacant land by the shore in which they were not crowded together; two or three rows deep, with scarcely an inch between them. And the costumes of these holiday folk! Or rather the lack of any costume in many instances. I can still recall the vision of the young lady in the emerald green pyjamas whom we met on the road on her way back to the camp with the morning milk. I'm surprised the horses didn't bolt. Then a few minutes later we were confronted by two peroxide-blonde beauties in very 'decoletée' turquoise blue shirts and the shortest of primrose yellow shorts who were strolling along with cigarettes between their carmine-tinted lips.

We stopped for a late breakfast just beyond Luss, and then without anything worth recording, reached Balloch. Late in the afternoon we came to Drymen. where at a farm on the banks of Endrick Water we found just the right quarters; nice friendly people and a good big field for the horses. Here we stopped for two nights. I took Tony into Glasgow so that he could do some business at a blacksmith's, for he had run out of nails. But owing to it being ' Fair Week ' most of the shops were closed and we must have walked several miles before we finally discovered one open.

We were quite sorry to leave that farm for we had seldom found ourselves treated so well. It was only a short distance from Drymen to Lennoxtown where we proposed to spend the week-end. Our route lay through Strathblane and Campsie. We passed through rich farming country, where in almost every field the men were at work putting up the hay.

Various enquiries in Lennoxtown, a drab looking industrial town, failed to produce camping ground, and I was advised to go on further. Finally, after yet more enquiries, we landed up at a farm just beyond the village of Milton of Campsie.

Here we seemed to be very far away from the Highlands. The scenery might be dull and tame when compared to the former; the Kilsyth Hills a poor substitute for the Grampians, but thank God! we were free from clegs and midges. It was indeed a blessed relief to escape from their murderous attacks.

Next day was Sunday. I walked back to Lennoxtown and heard Mass in the interesting little church, erected in 1846, to provide for the spiritual needs of the hundreds of poor Irish families who had settled in the town where they found work in the mills. The congregation was a large one and I found it difficult to get a seat. Lennoxtown was one of the first places in the industrial districts in the Lowlands where a Catholic church was built for the Irish.

These poor immigrants who flocked into Scotland at that period must have been a sturdy race to endure the hardships which they had to endure. They were forced to dwell in what were little better than rude hovels, hurriedly put up round the factories where they laboured. They sold their bodies for a mere pittance, and were obliged to work in foul and insanitary conditions from dawn to dusk; bullied and oppressed by their foremen and overseers, for in those days factory regulations were almost non-existent. There were no holidays; no Trade Union or Friendly Society benefits; no rightful share in citizenship. The only recreation for the men was in the public-houses which did a roaring trade, unchecked by present day regulations and closing hours. Except in rare instances there were no schools for the children, who were forced to start earning their living as soon as they were able.

By 1850 it is reckoned that at least a quarter of those employed in the industrial districts of the Lowlands were Irish. Their housing conditions were almost beyond belief, and it was no uncommon thing for a family of fifteen persons to dwell in a single room with only a small window to let in light. Here, so contemporary writers tell us, they would be found sleeping on beds of rotting straw and mouldy rags.

The lives of the Irish rural workers was no better, among whom disease was rampant. Their cottages had damp earth floors. The small windows seldom opened. In Glasgow, even as late as 1860, it was stated that 50 per cent. of the children born died under five years of age, and matters were no better in the country. This was how Scotland treated the poor refugees who had fled here to escape starvation in their own country. They were regarded as beasts of burden and treated worse than beasts by their employers, who were piling up vast fortunes from iron, steel, coal, shipbuilding and other industries.

Yet there was one thing to which the Irish held on to in spite of what they had to endure, and that was their religion. The supernatural virtues managed to flourish in spite of every obstacle. So in Lennoxtown, and later in hundreds of other grim forbidding-looking towns and villages, arose churches, built in most cases from the hard earned savings of the poorest of the poor. The æsthetic critic may sneer at these churches, but to those who can see beyond bricks and mortar they mean something much deeper. For thus out of great tribulation has the Faith been brought back to Lowland Scotland.

It has been raining all day and so I have had time to write up the events of the past week. We have spent a quiet Sunday at this farm and nobody has disturbed our solitude. There are times when the caravan seems an almost ideal home, and to-day has been one of them.

FIFTEEN

Carfin—Lanark—Broadfield Farm—Dumfries.

We left Milton of Campsie after breakfast, passing through
Kirkintilloch, a dull town with factories and bleach mills, and
so on across country, until we joined the main Stirling—
Carlisle road. We now entered industrial Lanarkshire, a
violent contrast to the mountains of Glencoe where we had
been a week ago. It was difficult to realise that Scotland could
contain such utterly different types of landscape within a few
miles of each other. But in everything Scotland is a nation of
far more extreme contrasts than England, not only in scenery,
but in social conditions and even in the temperament of its
people.

Skirting the mining town of Airdrie, with the smoke of its
many chimneys rising up to heaven like industrial incense, we
passed on through Chapelhall, a typical mining village, with a
Catholic church and large schools, testifying to the Irish origin
of many of its inhabitants. We found a camp site at a farm
not far from Newart Hill, a bleak windswept spot with an
extensive view over miles and miles of industrial towns and
villages, with more chimneys than one could count.

My reason for stopping here was to make a long overdue
pilgrimage to the now world-famous ' Grotto ' at Carfin, one
of the most extraordinary phenomena in 20th century Scotland.
It is just another example of what I have just stated that Scotland is essentially a land of extreme contrasts, for here in the
very heart of a district where Presbyterianism has held undis-
puted sway for over three centuries, and where it is rapidly
being supplanted by Communism; Karl Marx taking the place
of John Knox as the prophet and spiritual guide of the younger
generation, there should suddenly arise a vast Catholic

sanctuary which would excite comment even if it were in an essentially Catholic country like Belgium, Italy, or Poland.

I arrived in Carfin which in itself is about as unprepossessing a mining village as could be found anywhere in Great Britain. It consists of little else than a long straggling street of the most sordid looking two-storied houses, many of them empty, with boards fastened across the windows, owing to the danger of collapse from mines below the ground. In fact the whole of Carfin looks as if it might collapse suddenly one morning and nobody would bother about it.

Then on my right I noticed a wide open gateway—except that there were no gates—leading into what might have been the grounds of an exhibition or fair. At the entrance was a shop whose windows displayed what the French call ' objets de pieté.'

Until a year or two after the War few people outside Lanarkshire had ever heard of Carfin. It did not even possess a railway station. Then suddenly it became famous. The present rector, Canon Thomas N. Taylor, decided to build a replica of the grotto of Lourdes on some waste land in front of the church. It was put up by local miners who were then out of work. Pilgrimages were organised, quite small at first, then rapidly growing in size. Startling answers to prayer took place, even miracles, inexplicable by any human agency. To-day Carfin has become one of the most famous shrines in the world.

The original grotto has been extended, and now forms but a small part of what I can best describe as a large and beautifully tended garden, in which are scattered along its paths and gay borders of flowers, innumerable shrines of all the most ' popular ' saints of the moment. One meets St. Theresa of Lisieux and St. Philomena; one can descend into a Bethlehem grotto or ascend Mont' Alverna with St. Francis of Assisi. There is a striking Calvary, and Our Lady Star of the Sea, embowered in roses, stands on an island in the midst of a lake.

Having explored the sanctuary on my own I called at the

presbytery and was glad to meet Canon Taylor, to whose inspiration and enthusiasm is entirely due the Carfin which we find to-day. He welcomed me with the greatest kindness, and was almost indignant to hear I had left the caravan about a mile off. When I told him I must get back for supper as my companion was waiting for me, he ordered me to fetch him, and so I jumped on a bus, and to Tony's great surprise, informed him that he must come along with me as we were both invited to supper with the Canon.

After a pleasant meal, the Canon took us into the grotto; and when it had grown dark, switched on the flood lighting. The effect of the warm orange glow on the white marble statues was really most beautiful; even if fastidious critics would condemn it as being ' theatrical '—But why not? The flowers took on unexpected shades of colour of an almost exotic loveliness. Yet what was even more moving was to notice that even after 10 o'clock on a mid-summer night Carfin was not without its pilgrims. To watch the little groups kneeling in prayer on the hard ground made me feel I must be back at Lourdes, and it was almost impossible to believe that we were standing in what is geographically the very heart of Scotland. As I have already explained there are no gates at the entrance of the grotto : it remains open night and day, and what is very remarkable is that no attempt has ever been made by Prostestant mobs to desecrate the sanctuary. Perhaps they know too well what would be their fate if they dared to do so!

Sooner or later the little church, built in 1862, and now far too small to hold even the local congregation—for about 90% are daily communicants—still less the thousands of pilgrims who flock here on Sundays, will be replaced by a large and stately building in the traditional forms of Scottish-Gothic, for which designs have been prepared by Reginald Fairlie.

Tony and I returned to the caravan shortly after 11 o'clock. To myself, to have visited most of the famous shrines in Europe, Carfin was a surprise. To my companion, I think I am right in saying, it was a revelation of the privilege and responsibility which comes from being a Catholic.

The following morning we both went to Mass in the church. So crowded was it although it was merely an ordinary week-day, that Holy Communion had to be given throughout the Mass, otherwise the service would have taken about an hour. And this is merely what happens every day.

We spent most of the forenoon at Carfin, and did not leave the farm at Newart Hill until after midday. Passing through what thirty years ago was a busy mining district full of blazing furnaces and dingy looking collieries, we reached Carluke. To-day everything has changed owing to slump in major industries. Many of the pits are closed; the blast furnaces have been abandoned, and the slag heaps will soon be grass grown hillocks.

We stopped for tea beside the race course at Lanark, where I had time to make a rough sketch of the Catholic church, whose tall spire makes it a prominent landmark for miles round. It was not until 1859 that the Catholic religion took root again in this big market town, where only a few ruined arches are left of the pre-Reformation church dedicated to S. Mungo. As in so many other towns in Scotland the Presbyterians discovered that Catholic churches were not designed for their kind of worship, and very wisely from their point of view, erected new buildings in their place, allowing the old churches to fall into ruin.

It was Mr. Robert Monteith of Carstairs, a wealthy convert about the time of the Oxford Movement, who provided the funds to erect St. Mary's which was designed by George Goldie. But it was almost completely destroyed by fire in 1907. Messrs. Ashlin and Coleman of Dublin were called in to rebuild the church; the result being a characteristic example of their work in the Decorated style of Gothic.

The mission is in charge of the Vincentian Fathers, and adjacent to the church is a large hospital looked after by the

St. Mary's, Lanark.

Sisters of Charity. We met some of these good sisters in their white cornettes a few miles beyond Lanark. They were in company with a crowd of boys, for in addition to the hospital, they also maintain a big orphanage.

Passing under Tinto Hill, in connection with which I recited the well known old verse to my companion. It runs as follows :

"Be a lassie na'er so black
Gin she hae na any siller.
Set her up on Tinto tap
The wind will blaw a man till her."

But this afternoon there was no wind blowing over "Tinto tap"; a sultry heat hung over Clydesdale, and it would have needed more energy than either of us could muster to climb its summitt, no matter how much silver the lassie might have had to give us.

Catholic indeed was St. Isidore's Farm, Broadfield, up whose long drive the caravan rumbled about 8 p.m. Jack and Bill looked askance at the mass of red and white flowers placed around the statue of the Sacred Heart which was enough to tell us we had not mistaken our destination.

This 200 acre farm, beneath Tinto Hill, within quarter of a mile of the Clyde, was bought a few years ago by the Scottish Catholic Land Association, in order to carry out a long cherished plan of training and settling young men on the land.

The scheme, being new and original, was mistrusted and criticised by many Catholics, but it had the support of the present Archbishop of Glasgow. At his suggestion the farm was placed under the patronage of the 12th century Spanish farm-labourer, St. Isidore. Its first director was the Rev. John McQuillan, D.D. His indefatigable personality and enthusiasm for the work; his unquenchable efforts to prove to Scottish Catholics that this scheme is no mere day dream, in the face of a multitude of difficulties, opposition, as well as lack of financial supports, eventually proved more than his strength could stand. Since our visit to St. Isidore's Fr.

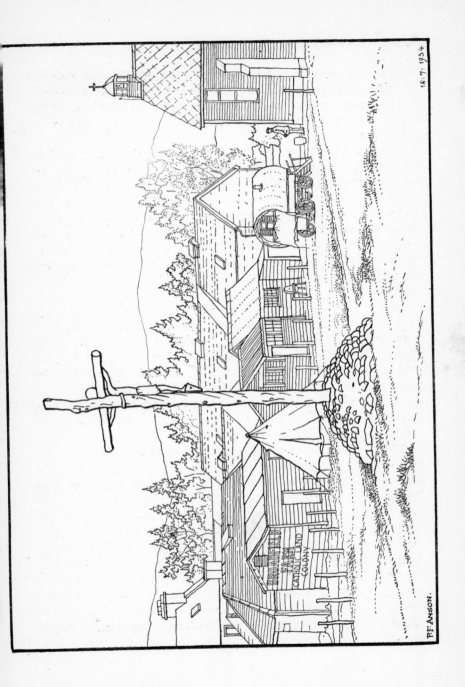

Broadfield Farm, Symington.

McQuillan has been forced to resign after a bad breakdown in health. Like so many other ' Land Colonies ' in Great Britain, St. Isidore's has come to an end, and the farm has been given up. The ideal is a splendid one, but it seems difficult to make it succeed.

We remained here two days; enough to give us an idea of the life on the farm, which included not only training in practical farming but also in practical Catholicism. I vividly recall the scene within the dimly lit chapel the last night we were here; the lads listening intently to their director who was giving them an instruction in plain chant; and at the same time explaining the inner meaning of the Sunday Vespers psalms. Then night prayers were said, after which we and the lads retired to bed.

Our road now led us up Clydesdale. As we passed through the villages of Lamington and Abington that morning I wondered what sort of welcome we should have received here during the 17th and 18th centuries, for this district was then famous as being the headquarters of the Baillies, one of the most powerful gipsy tribes in Scotland. The Baillies and Faas gave the title of king and queen to their reigning chiefs. The names of their ancestors are to be found in the treaty made with the gipsies by James V in 1540.

William Baillie of Lamington became notorious about the close of the 17th century. According to Mr. Simpson, author of the *History of the Gipsies*, whose grandfather knew him intimately, " Baillie was the handsomest, the best dressed, the best looking, and the best bred man he ever saw. He generally rode one of the best horses the kingdom could produce, he himself attired in the finest scarlet, with his greyhounds following him, as if he had been a man of the first rank. He acted the character of the gentleman, the robber, the sorner, and the tinker, whenever it answered his purpose. He was considered, in his time, the best swordsman in all Scotland." He claimed to be a bastard son of one of the Baillies of Lamington, an old

Border family, only his mother being a gipsy. Yet it is much more probable that he was descended from Towla Bailyow, who was one of the 16th century gipsies who rebelled against John Faa, ' Lord and Earl of Little Egypt.'

But we did not meet this romantic figure in his scarlet, or his greyhounds, although I should not be surprised if his ghost still haunts Clydesdale after dark. It would have been an exciting experience if William Baillie and his followers had surrounded our caravan as is recorded of a certain pedler on this very road over which we were travelling. If they had done so I hope we should have been treated in the same generous manner. The pedler was ordered to stop and lay out his packs on the ground. Baillie then unsheathed his sword, and with its point traced a circle round the terrified man; commanding his followers to remain outside the circle which he entered himself. Having examined the contents of the packs, he helped himself to the more valuable articles. The pedler imagined that he was ruined. But to his great surprise, Baillie then produced his purse, and handed over a sum of money which far exceeded the actual value of the articles he had retained. The pedler was allowed to continue his journey, and ever afterwards praised the gentlemanly behaviour of ' Captain Baillie,' as he called him.

Baillie was often arrested and brought to trial for ' sorning, pickery and little thieving '; and even banished the country. On more than one occasion he was condemned to be hanged, but the sentence was commuted in each instance. In the end he he was killed in a fight with another gipsy. Mr. Simson tells us that a century later William Baillie's descendants still swarmed over the Scottish Lowlands.

We had lunch a mile beyond Crawford, then turned right, taking a lonely road where we met very little traffic, through smooth green hills which provide ideal grazing for sheep. I had no idea of the peaceful beauty of this country which was all new ground to me.

Reaching the summit of Dalveen Pass after a long climb, we entered Dumfries-shire. The narrow road descends from here into Nithsdale. About 8 o'clock we came to one of those typical lowland farms; its white washed byres and barns gleaming in the light of the setting sun; everything scrupulously clean and tidy. The farmer willingly allowed us to stop the night in a field. We had several curious visitors after supper; a crowd of children who wanted to examine everything inside the caravan; also a peacock whose harsh shreak gave Jack and Bill quite a shock. They stopped grazing and stared at him. Never in their lives had they seen such an astonishing sight.

The following morning was showery and it was raining when we started off again soon after 7 o'clock. Past the farm of Ellisland, where Burns wrote "Tam o' Shanter" and "To Mary in Heaven," upon one of whose window panes he scratched "An honest man's the noblest work of God," we reached Lincluden Abbey. It was sad to see the red sandstone columns and arches of this 12th century Benedictine nunnery in ruins.

But the Benedictine Nuns have returned to the district, and a few miles further on we beheld the large priory at Maxwelltown, a suburb of Dumfries. It was erected by Baroness Herries in 1884 as an act of reparation for the sacrileges committed in Scotland at the Reformation. The imposing group of red sandstone buildings, designed by Peter Paul Pugin, stand on the very spot where Mass vestments and other objects connected with Catholic worship were burnt by the Reformers. This is the only Convent of Benedictine nuns in Scotland.

We crossed the river Nith, and having asked the way, eventually found St. Joseph's College, one of the most important Catholic Schools in Scotland, in charge of the Marist Brothers. The Brother Superior had already written to inform me that we should be welcome. He came with us to the playing fields,

St. Andrew's Cathedral, Dumfries.

on the outskirts of the town, where there was plenty of space for Jack and Bill to roam about. We parked the caravan in a quiet sheltered corner, and here we stopped from Saturday evening until Monday morning.

I made a sketch of St. Andrew's Cathedral, in which I found bits of almost every known style of architecture. The earliest portion of this curious building dates from 1813, and is Grecian in inspiration. Subsequent architects have experimented with both Gothic and Romanesque. There is an ornate reredos with fluted columns on either side of a copy of Vandyck's painting of the Descent from the Cross.

The Romanesque chapel at St. Joseph's College, erected by Charles Ménart as a War Memorial, possesses many interesting features. Like most of his work it is original and striking.

SIXTEEN

Gretna—Holme Eden Abbey—Penrith—Brough—Scorton—Ugthorpe—the end of our pilgrimage.

We left Dumfries on Monday morning and took the main road for Carlisle. This was our last day in Scotland. We had crossed the Border just over two months ago, and as I have related, had gone through some interesting, and often painful, experiences. Both Tony and myself were now beginning to feel just a little weary of travelling, and were looking forward to being back again in Yorkshire within ten days or so.

Hay-making was in progress in the fields along the road. We passed many large and prosperous looking farms and had our midday meal near Ruthwell, where I had a look at the famous Anglo-Saxon cross. The weather was showery and close. The horses seemed to be feeling tired as well as their drivers.

It was raining hard as we jogged through long main street of Annan, where I paid a brief visit to the little Catholic church. Then the sun came out and the clouds rolled away.

The Catholic church at Eastriggs which we came to a few miles beyond Annan seemed to belong rather to the plains of Lombardy than to Dumfries-shire. Like its companion, St. Ninian's, Gretna, of which I made a sketch, it was erected during the Great War when both these hitherto peaceful villages were suddenly transformed into busy centres for making munitions. Vast factories arose as if by magic, and ' garden cities ' were laid out to provide accommodation for the thousands of workers. The government also built churches for most of the chief religious bodies, and employed good architects. C. E. Simmons deserves high praise for his achievement at Gretna where it is a surprise to come upon one of the

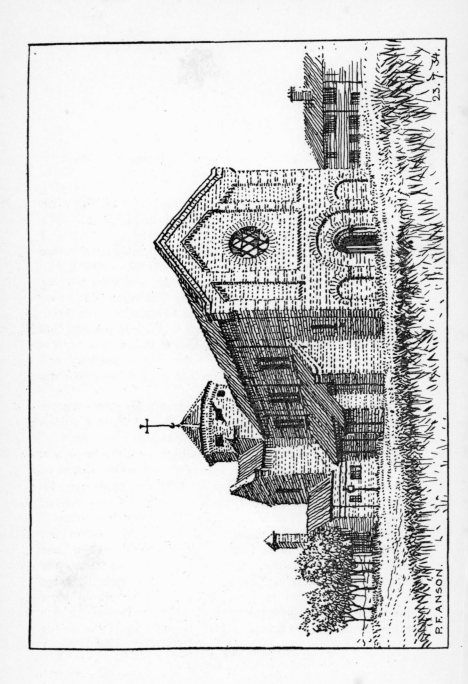

St. Ninian's Gretna.

most attractive modern Catholic churches in the whole of Scotland. The cordite factories have mostly been pulled down, and to-day Gretna and Eastriggs have a somewhat abandoned look.

I managed to find camping ground at the ' last farm in Scotland,' for at the end of the field in which the horses grazed was the stream which marks the border between the sister nations. It overlooks what used to be called the ' Debateable Land,' a stretch of flat marshes and moor over which English and Scots border-raiders used to quarrel during the Middle Ages.

Tony went off to have a look at the famous blacksmith's in Gretna village, where so many runaway marriages took place in bygone years. It has now become a show place for tourists and trippers. As is well known hundreds of couples, young and old, used to take advantage of the Scottish law, by which a simple declaration before two witnesses is enough to legalise their status as husband and wife.

While we were sitting outside the caravan after supper, a beautiful rainbow appeared in the sky above the distant mountains of Cumberland, which lay to the south across the silvery water and gleaming mud flats of the Solway Firth.

"That ought to be a good omen for the homeward journey," remarked my companion. "I feel sure we shall have no more bad luck, for the rainbow's in England and not in Scotland, and that's where we're making for to-morrow."

We left Allisonbank Farm about 9 o'clock, feeling that we could afford a longer rest than usual as we had only a short journey ahead of us that day. Crossing Sark Bridge we bade farewell to Scotland and entered England once more.

Near Floriston we met a party of young men pushing a cart, upon which was the strange inscription ' Methodist Friars.' I should like to have stopped and found out exactly what were the aims and objects of these Wesleyan followers of St. Francis.

Why is it I asked myself that the real friars—by which I mean the Franciscan and Dominican Orders—have ceased to be itinerant preachers? Why cannot they emulate these Methodist ' *fraticelli* ' and once more go out into the highways and byeways? There is plenty of scope for them in Scotland.

Carlisle did not detain us very long, and after a brief visit to the well designed Catholic church, a large Perpendicular Gothic building, we escaped from the busy streets of the city on to the Newcastle road. Having found a quiet spot we stopped and had lunch.

About 3 o'clock we turned in at the lodge gates of Holme Eden Abbey, one of the seven abbeys of Benedictine nuns which exist in England to-day. We drove up to the front door where I rang the bell and was shown into the parlour. The Lady Abbess gave me a most friendly welcome, and told me the caravan could be parked in the drive, for as she explained, all the nuns were eager to have a look at it. And she was right. The ' enclosure wall ' only consisted of a low wire fence. An hour or so later, while preparing tea, we were surprised by the sound of women's voices ,and on looking out beheld the whole community on the other side of the fence. They wanted to know every sort of thing—where we slept, where we cooked, and where was the larder, etc. ,etc. Their only regret was that they were not allowed to jump over the fence and step inside.

These Benedictine nuns who now occupy the mansion of Holme Eden, formerly the property of the Liddell family, removed here from Fort Augustus in 1921. They were founded by Abbot Leo Linse about fifty years ago. Their buildings were small and inconvenient, although few enclosed convents in Great Britain could boast such a lovely situation. In spite of many advantages gained by their removal to Cumberland, I realised when talking to the nuns, whom I used to know when they were at Fort Augustus, that they often look back with regret to their Highland home among the mountains.

Holme Eden Abbey.

Jack and Bill were allowed to enter the enclosure, and grazed in one of the fields. Both Tony and myself much enjoyed our brief visit to Holme Eden, and were grateful to Abbess Cecilia Carmont for her hospitality, both to ourselves and to the horses. I hope they appreciated their grass as much as we did the meals set before us by the nuns.

I served the Conventual Mass the following morning; break-fasting with the priest, a Dominican Father, who was staying here. During the forenoon I was occupied in making a sketch of the little Gothic church in the adjacent village of Warwick Bridge, a delightful example of Augustus Welby Pugin's work at its best, complete with rood-screen. This is an old Catholic mission, dating from about 1719. It has always been served by Benedictine monks, so there is a good reason why Holme Eden should have come into the possession of Benedictine nuns.

We drove away from the abbey after lunch. We passed through the village of Wetheral, and soon after this, on joining the main road from Carlisle to Penrith, had our last glimpse of Scotland as we surmounted a ridge from which there was an extensive view northwards.

There was nothing to complain of about the surface of this great broad highway, only we found the continual switchback ups and downs rather tiring, at least the horses did. Soon the distant mountains of the Lake District appeared on our right; Helvellyn, Skiddaw, and Saddlebank, being easily distinguished from the rest.

We passed a number of houses advertising ' night accom-modation,' ' bed and breakfast,' and ' camping ground,' but didn't think they would be much good to us. Finally, about 7 p.m. we came to a large farm which looked more promising. Just as I had reached the front door a motor stopped, and a man got out and joined me. It seemed that he and his party required ' beds and breakfast ' whereas we only needed ' camping ground.' The girl who answered the door said we could certainly put the horses in one of the fields, but seemed quite distressed that we should prefer to sleep under the roof of the caravan instead of in a bedroom at the farm. I bought half a dozen eggs and a pint of milk to console her, and these came in useful for supper and breakfast.

When we awoke next morning we found it was raining hard and a strong west wind blowing. It looked as if we were in for a wet day. We got away from the farm soon after seven, and stopped in Penrith to do some shopping, where I also visited the small Gothic church, built in 1850. It replaced a chapel, little more than a room, which had been opened in 1833.

We breakfasted close to Brougham Castle, and then went on again through Temple Sowerby to Appleby. From here to Brough there were bad hills all the way, the roads having a nasty ' slape ' surface, as my Yorkshire companion described it.

About 6 p.m. we found camping ground at a farm near Brough; one of those typical ' north-country ' stone farms of uncompromising appearance—built, so it would seem, to with- stand winter gales and snow storms.

Once again it was raining when we arose the following morning. The streets of Brough were more like mountain torrents as the caravan passed through this little town of grey stone houses. But an hour or so later the rain ceased, and the sun came out. Our road was one continual climb, but Jack and Bill managed the long ascent without much difficulty. It was not until well after midday that we reached the summit of the pass and arrived at the stone marking the boundary between Westmoreland and Yorkshire, some 1,568 feet above sea level. The view from here is magnificent. To the west the mountains of the Lake District; to the east rolling moor- lands, stretching away to the far distant Cleveland Hills.

The wind had increased to almost the force of a gale. Fortunately it was behind us, and the caravan was blown along the road across Bowes Moor. We stopped that night at a farm two or three miles the other side of Bowes.

And a restless night it was, for the gale became worse after we had gone to bed. The caravan swayed and creaked. I began to get nervous that a bough of a tree might be blown off and fall on the roof, or that even the tree itself might come crashing down on us. But fortunately no such disaster occurred. Accompanied by frequent heavy showers we drove on. crossed Greta Bridge, and followed the old Roman road which scarcely swerves an inch out of the straight line for nearly seven miles until it joins the Great North Road at Scots Corner. Through many winding lanes and corn fields we eventually reached the village of Scorton.

Here we spent the week-end, in a field belonging to the Brothers of St. John of God who run a large hospital for incurable cases. Most of the brothers are French and they established their hospital in Scorton in 1880. The original block of buildings had originally served as a convent for the Poor Clare nuns who are now at Darlington. Br. Flavien showed us all over the hospital; a large modern building containing 150 beds. This self-sacrificing work carried on by the Brothers is supported almost entirely by voluntary contributions.

We left Scorton early on Monday morning, and so eager were we by this time to reach the end of our journey that we were determined not to waste any precious moments on the roads. So we hurried onwards, if four miles an hour, which was about the average speed of the horses, can be described as ' hurried.'

There was little to interest us as we rumbled along over the dead level plain of central Yorkshire. This landscape, unless one has a professional knowledge of farming, can become very monotonous. We passed through the old market town of Yarm, one of the old Yorkshire Catholic missions, with a Gothic church designed by Hadfield and Goldie in 1860.

220

St. Mary's, Yarm.

A few miles beyond we found ourselves at a cross-roads. Turning right we were back again on the same road we had last traversed on May 1st, just twelve weeks ago. It seemed far more like twelve years. Past the blacksmith's shop in Marton, and then through the same winding lane that brought us to the same farm beyond Nunthorpe where we had spent our first night in what was then our ' new ' wagon. To-day it was no longer new, and its outside paintwork had already begun to look rather worn and shabby. The farmer and his wife seemed quite surprised to see us again, and found it hard to believe we had really got as far as the north of Scotland and back again in three months.

We left Nunthorpe after an early breakfast. The road was quite familiar to both of us for the rest of the journey. There was no need for us to stop in Guisborough. This morning ' Blue Bank ' caused us no alarm as it had done in February, when we were on our way north from the Thames Valley. Since we had exchanged the ' Portiuncula ' for a lighter van we had ceased to bother about hills. Unless they were absolute precipices Jack and Bill were fairly certain to climb them. No fatal accident, such as the breaking of a shaft, impeded our progress on the moorland road, which to-day looked very different to what it did on that wild stormy evening when I had been left alone here for over twelve hours. Then the colouring had been dull brown and grey, to-day the heather was in bloom, and on either side of the road lay a rolling carpet of purple.

At last we came to the signpost pointing the way to Ugthorpe. The horses seemed to realise that they were nearing home at last. Their speed for the past five miles had been amazing. They needed rather to be held back than urged forward. It was about 4 o'clock when we drove into the yard of the Black Bull Inn.

So ended the Caravan pilgrimage. I had every intention of

starting off again on another long tour after a few months rest. Quite a number of priests had written to me asking when I should be able to draw their churches. Reverend Mothers had invited me to sketch their convents, and were eager to make the acquaintance of the now two celebrated horses Jack and Bill. It really seemed as if I might go on wandering round Great Britain indefinitely, so long as there remained subjects to sketch and a paper which would publish the drawings. But as a matter of fact the cost of this mode of life exceeded the regular payments I was receiving. I realised I was actually losing money instead of making any profit. On a rough calculation our total weekly expenses worked out at between £3 and £5. This included ' board and lodging' for my companion and myself; the two horses, together with sundry items such as shoeing the horses, repairs to harness, and general wear and tear. Actually the total sum was less than I should have paid if I had been on my own, travelling by train and staying in hotels or lodgings.

I ventured to point out to the *Universe* what unique publicity was afforded by the caravan; how it was a never-ending source of interest and curiosity in every town and village, or along the country roads. For this reason I had hoped that the paper might see its way to adopt the caravan as a sort of ' mascot.' I stated that I would be willing to adorn the sides of the wagon with some such words as ' READ THE UNIVERSE '; or decorate the roof with a large papier-maché globe surmounted by a Papal Tiara, reminiscent of the ' Open Bible ' which distinguishes Mr. Kensit's Protestant evangelist motor-caravan devoted to fighting Popery! A friend, to whom I mentioned this scheme, suggested a gramophone and loud-speaker as an additional means of obtaining publicity. " It could play ' Faith of Our Fathers ' and ' God bless Our Pope,' " he remarked!

But my suggestions did not rouse the same enthusiasm as I had anticipated, and they were turned down. Who can tell but that such blatant methods of advertisement might have even decreased the circulation of a newspaper instead of increasing it? Anyhow this would seem to have been the opinion of those who knew more about the value of publicity methods than I did.

So much to my regret I now realised that there was no alternative but to get rid of Jack and Bill, and to sell the caravan. Tony had no difficulty in finding purchasers for the horses, for both of them were now in such fine condition, thanks to the care he had devoted to them, that anybody would have been glad to buy such beasts. It was sad to say good-bye to Jack and Bill. I only hope they found good homes and have been well looked after by their new masters.

Having sold Jack I felt I had better sell the van as soon as possible. Rather to my surprise I got a good offer within a few days from a neighbouring gipsy, who was also willing to take Bill. Tony and I cleared out all our private possessions; removed mattresses, pillows, and blankets, kitchen utensils and crockery (i.e., the enamelled tin plates and mugs on which we had eaten our meals all the time we were on the road). We took away everything that was not actually a fixture, so that when the job was done, the interior of the wagon looked very desolate and bare.

Then, putting Bill into the shafts, we set off from Ugthorpe for the last time. So depressing was the interior of the wagon that I preferred to walk, rather than sit and contemplate the surroundings which had been our home.

At a given spot on the main road, about three miles from Whitby, where one looks down into the deep valley of the Esk, and far across the rolling moors almost to Scarborough, we met the future owner of the van. I presented Bill with a lump of sugar as a parting gift—remembering his weakness in this direction. The gipsy gave me the money for the horse and wagon; then jumping up on to the seat above the shafts, took the reins in his hands, and drove away.

Tony and I walked back to Ugthorpe; both of us realising that a chapter in our lives had ended, and uncertain of the future which lay before us.